05/27/2015

ONLY HUMAN STORIES
OF
LOVE & LOSS AMONG MORTALS

Winchinchala

Winchinchala is the first-born daughter of Seawolfe, Sagamore of a Wôpanâak (Wampanoag) Indian Nation and Joy, of Austrian/Irish heritage. Studies, work and curiosity have taken her to distant ports in the world for weeks, months and, at times, years. Its peoples, their diverse cultures, histories, myths and her life experiences are woven throughout her stories. Many of her characters have been affected by familial dysfunction and trauma, areas with which, she confesses she is "sadly too familiar." She is an active advocate for destigmatizing depression and suicide through education communication and tolerance.

Winchinchala is a graduate of Columbia University in the City of New York where she earned B.A. in social anthropology and Germanic languages and an MFA in Film/Writing. She won the Warner Brothers' Award for THE TEA PARTY a screenplay and her play REMOTE MANwas runner up for the prestigious New England Clauder Playwriting Competition. Prior to a decade as a professor at Berklee College of Music, she spent one teaching at Boston University. Over the years, she has run independent creative writing workshops, given cross-cultural presentations, and coached voice for actors at The Actors' Workshop. Currently she writes full time.

Only Human, Short Stories of Love & Loss Among Mortals is a collection of fiction. Names, characters and incidents are the product of the author's imagination. Any resemblance to actual events, locales or persons, living or dead, is entirely coincidental.

Printed in the United States of America.
Library of Congress Cataloging-in-Publication Data

ISBN 978-1-889768-38-0 Winchinchala

Only Human Stories of Love & Loss Among Mortals
/Winchinchala.

Cover design by Winchinchala based on *El primer beso de Adan y Eva*, Salvador Viniegra y Lasso de la Vega (1891) in Museo del Prado in Madrid

2nd Edition: People With Wings Edition:

10 9 8 7 6 5 4 3 2 1

Also by *Winchinchala*

FICTION/ NON-FICTION BOOKS

SEXY SOLITARY SUICIDE 2nd Edition (Self-
Help/Psychology/History)
THE LIFE AND LOVES OF MARINER JACKIE VIK
A LITTLE CITY INDIAN IN THE 1950'S
CALLIOPE, AN UNFINISHED DIARY
NEENEEMOOSHA SWEETHEART

TV /SELECTED SCREENPLAYS

SEINFELD Episode: "Schleppen Feathers" (1997)
REMOTE MAN, a play in three acts,
(New England *Clauder Playwriting Competition,* Runner up
1995, ©1990/publication 2002)
SAVING GRACE (Screenplay)
THE TEA PARTY (Winner of Warner Bros. Award)

VIDEOS (writer/producer/director)
Winchinchala
THE EMPRESS DOWAGER'S ROBE (2001)
REFLECTIONS OF AN EVENING (1999)
YOUNG LOVERS' CHRISTMAS COWBOY CAVIAR (1998)

DEDICATED TO:

Dad, Seawolfe & his wife M.A.,
& my brothers Bert & J.

CONTENTS

Artwork and Photographs

Book front cover art: collage by Winchinchala based on *El primer beso de Adan y Eva* by Salvador Viniegra y Lasso de la Vega (1891).

***

Morning Mist in Colorado: Photo by Winchinchala (p. 2).
Detail of *Der Kuss*, 1907 1908, Gustav Klimt (p. 20).
Arcangelo & the Ponderosa Pines: Original drawing by Winchinchala 1972-2011 (p. 24).
Through the Latticework: derivative/collage w/ sources: *The Mirror*, Frank Bernard Dicksee, 1896 & *Portrait of Prince Alexey Kurakine*: by Ludwig Guttenbrunn, 1801 (p. 28).
Confessional carving Church of St. Sebastien, Nancy, France. Photo by Vassil (p. 29).
Titian – Artemis (Diana) and Actaeon, Titan, 1156 National Gallery, London. (p.34)
Sous les Laurels : Etienne Dinet 1891 (p. 46).
Kama Sutra detail (p. 58).
Detail and Derivative of color photo of *Gombey Dancers* performing in Kings Square, St. George Bermuda by Captain Tucker, 2004 (p.79).
The Picnic Table, unknown (94).

i

Woman in Bar, collage, Winchinchala (p.104).
Typewriter Jam: unknown, Public Domain (p. 130).
Tom's Diner. Photo by Rick Dikeman – (2000) Derivative by Winchinchala (p. 133).
Vintage Absinthe Poster (p. 138).
Studio 54 VIP (original gold) (p. 141).
Winter Snow in NY, Collage by Winchinchala, Source Library of Congress, Prints & Photographs Division, Carl Van Vechten Collection, [reproduction number, e.g., LC-USZ62-54231] (p. 147).
WWII Maritime Poster (p. 152).
Vintage post card from Greece (p. 179).
Photo of gulls, Winchinchala (p. 180).
Illustration from Adam's Diary, Mark Twain, 1904 (p. 190).

Notes to the Reader:

Length: This second edition includes all the stories in the first as well as Winchinchala's short story, "Aeschylus on Ocean Avenue" and "Excerpts from Adam's Diary" by Mark Twain.

Language: *Only Human Short Stories* take place in different decades, and the language reflects the time period. For example, the pronoun "he" may be more predominant and words such as chick or girl have been used rather than woman.

Images: Winchinchala has drawn and painted since an early age. Her ability to see a scene came in handy when she studied screenwriting, and readers have often commented that her writing is very visual. She said, "In addition putting phenomenal research tools at one's fingertips, the best thing about the internet is that it has made people better readers of pictures. I cannot imagine writing without images. They go together."

Image quality: In order for books to print-on-demand, a cookie cutter format is required, so with the flick of a button the inkjet printers anywhere on the planet will generate a particular book. The printing press and weight of the paper dictate the quality of the image, which, at this time, is not high. For our books, we had to abandon certain images, take liberties to lighten or otherwise alter them. Each was chosen with great care by the author herself to accompany a poem or passage. Thank you for your understanding.

Inner Monologue: There are different approaches to representing inner monologue, meaning dialogue when a character speaks to him/herself. People With Wings uses italics, not quotes.
Our readers are smart; they will get it.
Punctuation of Poetry: is spontaneous or inspirational in style. She reacts to a vision or an emotion which overflows so powerfully that she must write it. She prefers to use spacing rather than punctuation, but sometimes returns to add punctuation.

Acknowledgements

~ I owe a special debt of gratitude to my father, Seawolfe & M.A., his wife of many decades.

~ Frank Tabata, Honolulu, Hawaii, a mysterious, kind-hearted crooner, often veiled in silence.

~ For their heartfelt encouragement and support: Lauren Hendrix, David Howland, Trey Stuvek, Maggie Martin (Jelenic).

~ John Courduvelis of Lexington, MA & Nemea, Greece. John, a gifted composer and singer who saved the stories from malicious viruses and gross operator error on more than one occasion. Of equal importance was his convincing that I should continue to continue.

~ Dr. N. whose wisdom, patience, generosity and humor help me to see myself in a brighter light, so I can continue writing and living.

Trying to figure out the meaning of life for ourselves is a complicated matter. Throw another person and add romance into the mix and the experience can become a dizzying quandary. From the time I was thirteen and noticed boys noticing me, I found attraction mysterious and the ritual of courtship frustrating and even a little annoying. Guidelines for kissing and petting were dictated by protocol and often interfered with love. According to the creation myth of Judaism, matching humans defied God Himself. After all, his initial pairing of the first lovers was between Adam and Lilith. She let it be known that she was not pleased about being appointed wife and child-bearer. Her defiance resulted in the Lord sending a band of angels to collect her and spirit her away. Thus, the legend goes, God decided to couple Adam with a woman literally created from his body, his rib in particular, to improve the possibility of a successful union. When poor, unsuspecting Adam was asleep, God took one of his ribs and fashioned Eve which must have been painful. Despite having been subjected to the clandestine procedure and enduring the famous apple-eating incident that angered God, Adam and Eve stayed together. "Adam's Diary," translated by Mark Twain is a comical account of how the couple grew accustomed to each other, overlooked idiosyncrasies and made their relationship with its inimical beginnings, work.

Is that how it is for all long-lasting relationships? My perspective has inspired friends and readers to ask me, "Why are you so cynical? Don't you believe in love?" For the record, I confess I do but not in society's happily-ever-after fairytale version. It is a tricky, chemical connection interwoven with compromise, commitment and respect, and as most people know, it is an extraordinarily rare treasure. Coveting it, so many and blinded by infatuation or deliberately delude themselves into thinking they are in "love." Denial prevents them from admitting they decided on their partner because they were "tired of dating," some magic somehow (ahem) "got pregnant" at eighteen or forty-four, "didn't want to be alone" or incorrectly assumed great sex could be a solid foundation for love or something on which they could build true love. They move in together or perhaps marry and the high of those events vanquishes any doubts or misgivings, and they sail onto seas of optimism confident they will survive the many negative, unknown stressors in life.

Consciously and unwittingly, in putting the union first, one or the other partner may have compromised his/her aspirations. Bad personal habits and personality traits such as perpetually arriving late; overspending, leaving the top off the toothpaste, snoring like drunken water buffalo, revealing what's going to happen next in a film, overtly flirting or clinging to one's partner with ardent codependency are condoned, at least for a little while, a longer while if the sex is fanfriggin'tastic. In fact, a good sex has been known to trivialize even infidelity, mental cruelty and physical abuse, well, unless it is directed at the children or pets. (A woman I know actually divorced her husband after only six weeks because her husband cold-cocked her dog.) Couples find ways to stay in the relationship because coping with the familiar is more tolerable than admitting failure; facing being older alone, returning to loneliness, navigating the dreaded dating scene or the unknown. They have all heard the common sense advice that "You should marry your best friend," but that is trumped by the chemistry of attraction and the complexity of the psyche and people go for the heightened feelings and fantasy of romantic love which wasn't even part of Western culture until the dawn of the 14th century.

In those reverent days, the church upheld chastity. It had its hands wrapped firmly around masturbation and all carnal activity because sensual pleasure was a sin. The purpose of sex was procreation. Living up to that Christian ideal of man being "master of his domain" was a formidable challenge and continued to be so. Hundreds of years later that fact was brought home by the brilliant *Seinfeld* episode "The Contest" (11.18.1992). The four main characters, Jerry, George Kramer and Elaine bet on who could abstain the longest from "smiting the pink knight." The savvy, self-proclaimed, strong-willed Manhattanites threw in their hands in relatively short order. What chance did wandering minstrels, wenches and knights, who went commando, stand in the morally-impoverished, mead-soused milieu of yore?

Enter the written word. Eleanor of Aquitaine, wife of kings, Louis VII of France and Henry II of England, and her daughter, Marie, Countess of Champagne fell under the spell of chivalrous knights' verses. They were not rife with bawdy lust for noblewomen's bodies but praise for their unobtainable virtue cached beneath their numerous silken petticoats. This poetry esteemed not the act of lust but the beloved herself and held the suitor in an ever-constant state of despair and was perceived as an ennobling force and, according to historical sociologists, responsible for chaste, romantic love becoming idealized and popularized. Repression carried over well into the 17th century as is evidenced by its dour prudery, but by the 20th century everyone had grown weary of restraint and tastes swung in the other direction.

A Sub-genre of romantic writing emerged, bodice-rippers Their pages drip with sensuality steamy enough to make a Louisiana stripper blush, yet they make up a good 14% of all sales. Alas, writers write what they know and fantasize, and for me that is neither soft romance nor hard-core sex but tumultuous relations. The forces, sociological and psychological, thwarting or spurring the individuals' behavior and how it holds them in, often unhappy limbos, intrigue me incredibly.

For example, I knew a man named Thomas who had a beautiful Ficus tree in his New York City living room. They are difficult plants to grow, especially in an apartment, but he nurtured the puny sapling and it flourished. "Love" he boasted was the reason, and that was true. One brutally cold February when the electricity went out, he used his sick days to stay home, cover the tree with plastic and keep it warm with battery-powered heaters. "He sleeps with that damn tree more than me," his wife Pamela sniped. Years later, the Ficus inexplicably fell ill and dropped all of its leaves. Pamela flaunted her schadenfreude and bought a little rake for Thomas to "get the leaves off my silk carpet." He did, but he also made every effort to revive the tree. When healing and salvation were clearly impossible, he became inconsolably depressed. His friends consoled him as best they could and eventually helped him carry it down to the curb. They toasted in farewell and suggested he do the same with his "banshee of a wife" who they suspected of poisoning his beloved ficus. He agreed with them, but he stayed.

It seems her casual critical remarks had become frequent, and she freely punched him in front of their children. Sleeping in separate rooms, as they had for almost as long as he could remember, forced him to take his personal needs into his own hands to diminish the chances of his cheating on her which he thought was truly wrong. Of course, to achieve the desired "happy ending" to his manual romances, he employed pictures of women, fantasies online at first, then escalated to women in the flesh, but only for non-penetrating activities which as far as he was concerned were not technically having sex. Still, the guilt ate at him. When he finally told her he thought they should go to a marriage counselor, she stung him with her usual condescending criticism and blamed him for the collapse of the marriage. "You're the one with the problem. You go!" He did. It was helpful and enlightening, but according to the therapist, without her participation, there was no way to heal their union. Still, he chose to stay in the agonizing cesspool of lonely autoeroticism, negative emotions, and psychological abuse that hurt not only him but their children. The psychiatrist pointed out that their impressionable, young psyches were being subconsciously imprinted with the cold, loveless treatment he and his wife modeled. He shared that with his wife, yet both stayed in the marriage. As a result, the couple perfected the art of maintaining their existence, getting bills paid, taking the kids where they needed to go, communicating in snarky retorts. His friends watched him change and wanted their old friend back. They did not understand how Thomas, a guy who "could have had any woman he wanted," remained. Guesses included "the kids," "feeling sorry for her," she was "a good social match," "Hellfire between the sheets" or that it was "cheaper to keep her," as the old jazz song goes. To them, leaving Pamela, who he didn't love half as much as he did the ficus plant, should have been easy.

Truly elationships are complex and mysterious creatures that have lives of their own. They inspire my stories, including these in ONLY HUMAN SHORT STORIES OF LOVE & LOSS AMONG MORTALS.

Winchinchala
Boston, Massachusetts,
May 27, 2015

ONLY HUMAN STORIES
OF
LOVE & LOSS AMONG MORTALS

Happy Day

"Morning Mist" ©Winchinchala

Happy Day

I

Whenever the Ponderosa came up, Happy envisioned the, old TV western *Bonanza.* That fictional ranch in Nevada was occupied by Ben Cartwright and his three commitment-phobic, bachelor sons, Little Joe, Adam and Hoss. All the girls and, no doubt, a few boys, in Happy's youth had a crush on Little Joe, but she preferred Adam, the taller, older brother who had a deep voice and a confident swagger. Now and then Happy had a daydream in which she wore a flowing, calico dress while collecting wildflowers in a sun-drenched valley. Adam appeared and waved, and they would run, in cinematic slow motion, into each other's arms. As their lips met, a shot rang out. Blam! Adam's vigilant father, Ben had killed a wild cat before it was able to pounce on them. That sort of drama was what *Bonanza* was all about. That daydream was but one grain of sand that made up the beaches of distant and recent memories that ebbed and flowed into her thoughts. She wondered if her life would ever provide her any drama as thrilling as those of the wild west.

Her life had always been close to New York, even before she became an artist and the city her muse. Once an interviewer asked her why, and she answered that, "It's a grand man-made canyon that holds the entire diversity of humanity, perpetually evolving and changing, screaming in agony and delighting in ecstasy." Immersing herself in painting, as thoroughly as she did, gave rise to predictions in her circle that she would never marry; although she was well sought after.

Her latest was Elwood whose friends were similarly convinced he would remain alone because he too was consumed with a passion, managing the family investment firm with a long-term goal of building an offshore hedge fund. Happy and Elwood had both told the naysayers they were only waiting for "the right one to come along," the one who would understand their intense devotion to what they were doing, give them space and encourage their pursuits, no matter how disparate they might be. To everyone's surprise, each concluded the other "the one," and they become a dazzling couple with a quiet reputation for philanthropy, on everyone's guest list.

Happy was responsible for arranging their social schedule which was, most frequently, in the city but also in Palm Beach, Los Angeles and occasionally London, Paris or Venice. After a decade had rolled effortlessly by, Elwood mentioned adding Colorado to their world because an incredible opportunity that would bring him closer to his long term goal had landed in his lap. Even though it was in Colorado and not Nevada, images of Bonanza flowed in and incited a deep anxiety because part of the deal meant relocating in there. Neither Adam nor his father was there, just the mountain lion ready to pounce which pulsed a foreboding sense of doom through her veins.

"I don't want to be stuck in cowboy Colorado," she griped.

"What? You love Vail."

"I do. But visiting Vail and living in Ponderosa are very differ-

4

ent things."

Elwood spoke for a long time about why the move would be "an adjustment, but nothing we can't handle, and in the end, good," in a speech that sounded polished and rehearsed. Almost all the upsides were in his favor, but to be fair he wanted her to "go and have a look," before she made up her mind.

II

The company limo rolled into the range of lavender-grey Rocky Mountains shaded with great, evergreens nestled in the southwestern section of Colorado. There, they wandered to the top of a little grass-clumped ridge. A fine mist arose and gave the carpet of miniscule blue wildflowers beneath the trees the look of an impressionists painting. She turned to share her feelings with El, but he had already gone to the car where he sat texting, talking on the blue tooth, watching a screen, more involved with his work than her decision. He was relatively certain she would not want to live there because she was a dyed-in-the-wool urbanite, so he had serious doubts about their future together. He loved her as much as a man married to his career can love his wife, and he knew they were a perfect match of opposites whose differences complimented each other.

Elwood was aloof which Happy attributed to his upbringing in an environment of privileged and protocol that molded a conventional exterior around him, but it balanced hers, which he identified as artistic, impulsive and effulgent but "not too." Conformity was as essential an element to his success as connections, determination and savvy. So while he wanted a wife who was beautiful, he needed one who was interesting but not provocative; sensual but not sexy; skilled in conversing but not glabrous, just like the other wives. His partners were relocating to Colorado, and he had already decided he would follow whether Happy wanted to or not. Unbeknownst to her, Elwood had already consulted with an attorney and considered two replacements for the role of wife.

Jejune was a lissome knockout with whom he had a special connection and "phenomenal, mind-blowing sex." Enjoyable as her minx-like ways were, they could not off-set her inclination to booze that made her too free in public and her declaration that she "never wanted any children." He was willing to accept that from Happy, but had since changed his mind, and if he married again, children were a must. Then there was Julie, the sweet, divorced redhead composer he had met at a one of Happy's gallery openings eighteen months earlier. Their harmless flirtations escalated to the brink of consummation where their morals held them in check. He guessed she was about ten months his junior, and he saw how she lit up around kids. *She might be the one...well...the next one.* Suddenly the image of Julie's nipples hardening beneath her red silk blouse flashed in his mind, and he closed his eyes to better view them and the disarming vulnerability of her face which he thought unusually pretty. A kiss on the cheek from Happy brought him back to Colorado.

She pranced merrily into a spray of white, Rocky Mountain sunlight, and he thought about how easily they had traveled through time, how easy she was to be with. Happy had never made any demands on him or tried to change him in anyway. Now, he was asking to change her self in order to be able to fit into a whole new world. A twinge of pain stuck him from the guilt he suffered over cheating on her with Jejune and the closeness he felt for Julie. The edge of the return ticket to New York he had bought for Happy, in case she declined, stuck through his pocket and scratched his chest, but she didn't give him an opportunity to remove it. In the middle of the ground that would become their living room, Happy flung her arms out to the side. "So much space. All this nature. Wonderful, just wonderful." He caught her in a tender, embrace before she broke free and dashed up a hill whispering loudly, "Look! Deer!" He ambled along behind her envisioning his Denver skyline office. Happy prattled on about "log accents, chestnut floors, vaulted ceilings" and where she would put her studio for optimal light.

Elwood gave his input on the design of the house but left most of the input to Happy. She had an excellent rapport with the architect who suggested green options for light and energy in their location, but he tapped his shoe with excited interest when she mentioned she would "perhaps like mosaic walls, a fountain in a grand entryway" and "a balcony for each bedroom."

"A personal vista for each of the bedrooms?"

"Yes," Happy confirmed. "When guests visit they shouldn't ..."

"Be visible?" he interrupted with a chuckle.

"I was going to say, have to give up their privacy."

"Right."

∗∗∗

The trendy magazine *Exteriors Interiors* featured the Days home on its cover under the title, "A Ponderosa Palace." The lengthy article described it as "a magnificent work of art reflecting the couple's refined New England taste along with their reverence for the West's nature." Despite Happy's abundant efforts, Elwood received the lion's share of credit, and at work, that earned him the nickname of Mr. Palace. He was proud of the amusing sobriquet, his accomplished, adaptable wife and his "spectacular home whose every corner celebrates the vista of mountains and majestic pines." When she e-mailed Tristan, her brother, she attached a copy of the article from *Exteriors Interiors* and underlined the section which did mention her. "The Ponderosa Palace is occupied by financial executive Mr. Elwood Day and his wife, New York artist, Happy." She highlighted the word "artist" and drew a smiley face. Unlike Elwood, her brother had always encouraged her art, expressed keen interest and enlightening personal criticism.

Elwood was more interested in the status that came with her being an artist than her art. On the rare occasion that he asked about her work and she showed him, he invariably replied, "Very nice Happy." She didn't mind because beyond the word, "invest-ments," she neither understood what he did for a living nor felt the need to ask because as she told her friends, "He doesn't ask me to explain what I do." Happy painted for the joy, not for the compliments but when they came, the idea that what she had successfully transferred thoughts to canvas and communicate with a viewer excited her soul. Mention of her paintings in the article drew the attention of the well-connected few who gov-erned the West and Southwest arts scene, and just like that, she became a hit. Dealers called almost immediately and by the new year, they had installed Happy's "Abstract pinescapes" in venues in Colorado, New Mexico and California. She maintained a minimal staff that came but bi-weekly, to prevent distraction and allow her to get lost in her work.

III

Elwood was almost never at "the Palace." His commute was an hour and a half each way and he always seemed to be needed in person, so he rented an apartment in town. At first, the arrange-ment reinstated their early loving feelings for each other, and they met for sexy trysts, candlelight dinners and romantic visits to museums and the park in Denver. When Elwood's devoted secretary, Fanny called with the details of when and where Happy was to go, she tingled with excitement. Two years later, the arrangement seemed to be more for El's convenience. It was an imposition, an intrusion into her creativity. She complained to her brother Tristan that she was afraid she and El had "drifted too far apart. I can never call a meeting. It's all about him. I did my dating, and I thought I had a marriage, but..."

"Are you talking to him about that?"

"Yes, but...He doesn't want to quit his job, so..."

"What if you moved into Denver with..."

"No!"

"Okay. Don't yell. Look, I'm really not in a position to give you advice. Maybe a counselor would..."

"A counselor?" she burst out laughing. "El would never agree to that. What's a childless, aging wife to do?"

"Not beat herself up. Not believe she is a mind reader."

She agreed to attempt to talk to him. Running through a variety of possible scenarios, she decided on one that could lead them to an honest discussion and a counselor, though she predicted his possible replies would be, "I don't see the problem," or "I don't have time for that."

Determined to try, she planned to bring up her discontent when they had their next rendezvous, the coming Tuesday. She waited for him in the sophisticated, historic Brown Palace Hotel's bar tingling with adolescent anxiety. Elwood was characteristically late, so she took advantage of the time to touch up her make-up. In the powder room, there were two women; one appeared to be in her sixties, the other in her early twenties. All faced the mirror. The older powdered her nose and captured a strand of silver hair which had escaped a heavy dose of lacquer and looked down at her hands while she washed them. The younger adjusted the spaghetti-strap of her dress hanging loosely over her slim, firm, bra-less body, then bent forward to toss volume into her mane. Happy glanced from one to the other, and then looked at herself. Small crêpe paper crow's feet fanned out from the sides of her large hazel eyes. One aggravating parenthesis was forming on the left side of her mouth. The slightest of jowls drooped around the curve of her jaw. To her own over-critical eye, she looked weary, though she had slept well. Booze, her frequent companion, had been lapping at her youthful veneer. However her spa-maintenance regiment had, thus far, kept her middle-age from announcing itself too loudly.

"What's that?" asked the young woman watching as she dabbed cold water around her eyes.

"Just water. It perks up the skin."

"Oh." The girl presented her youthful cheek to the mirror in the harsh bathroom light and concluded, "I am perky enough," pushed up her breasts, and gave her a coy little wink before she sashayed out.

Happy outlined her mouth with lip liner, made a mental note to indulge in one of her clay beauty masks and another note to drink less... *starting tomorrow, can't be tonight.* Tonight, she foresaw the dramatic tragedy of her vanishing marriage transforming into an erotic escapade with the help of a few cocktails.

The last time she and El stayed at the Brown Palace, they had unleashed their inhibitions enough to succumb to their desires on the deserted roof in plain sight of the full moon. Supported partly by the rough brick wall and partly by Elwood, her limbs were free and her eyes open to a rocking view of the night-blackened mountains penetrating the star-dusted sky.

"God, it's like doing it in Heaven," she whispered when he helped her to the ground.

He smiled and promised they would "do it in Heaven again sometime soon."

That was almost a year ago Saturday.

We'll start anew tonight, she told herself,

Desire ached along her inner thighs. She hated waiting and had even arrived late to bypass the discomfort it brought. On the stool, she fidgeted in her purse for her cell phone which, to her dismay, was emitting a dead battery beep. She placed it on the bar and then heard her name.

"Mrs. Day?" The maître d'hôtel who was familiar with she and El approached with, "Excuse me Mrs. Day, telephone."

Fanny, El's secretary, was on the line. "I tried your cell, but it went right to voicemail and the home number went ..."

"No worries Fanny," she sighed. "Why is El late? I'm...?"

"I'm sorry but they had to go to London because..."

"They?" Happy interrupted.

Fanny corrected herself, "I mean Mr. Day. And he will call when he gets there. He is staying at ..."

"Thank you."

The details didn't interest her. No longer in waiting mode,

10

she settled at the bar to slake her disappointment. A tall man with square shoulders in a perfectly tailored, chalk-stripe suit had taken the chair next to her. The faintest scent of his cologne pulled her eyes toward him. Feeling her gaze, he swiveled around to rest his weight on the chair arm and flashed a handsome grin.

"Long day?"

Politely, she nodded.

"Not to sound too corny but, what's a girl like you doing in a place like this?"

"Waiting for my husband."

"Are you?" he asked undeterred.

In order to leave the bar which had become quite crowded, Happy had to slide off the stool by the man. The space was tight. He didn't move. His breath was warm on her head; his starched shirt was stiff on her face. They were so close; she could feel his firm warm muscles beneath the fine soft fabric of his shirt and pants. A chemical attraction held them in a flirtatious gaze that they held for a few seconds.

"I'm Lemminkäinen Markuksentytär," he uttered in a voice brimming with genuine charm.

"Really?" she giggled in amusement.

"Really. It's my name. It's Finnish.

"And so are we."

"Cute. Everyone calls me Lempi. And you are..."

Deliberately, she placed the palm of her left hand flat on his chest. Her wedding ring sparkled in the quasi bar light.

"Still Missus."

He guffawed and stepped back to allow her to smooth by him. His eyes traced her shapely legs up to her curvy bottom as she tottered tipsily toward the door. Her phone beeped on the bar, and he grabbed it and rushed after her.

"Missus!" he called out to her in the cab. He placed the phone in her outstretched palm with his business card. "I think this is yours?"

"It is. Thank you."

The traffic light turned green and the cab took off. Out of the back window, she saw Lempi wave. After turning his card over about a hundred times, she flicked it out the window.

At home at the Ponderosa, she buzzed around in her slinky dress unable to shake off the aggravation Elwood's cancellation had infused in her. "Idiot! Coward! Why hadn't he called himself?" For a split second, she regretted discarding Lempi's card. She Googled the name. It read "Lempi means love in Finnish," and she laughed. A pitcher of Margaritas soused the sharp ends of her nerves. She called Tristan.

"Pick up the phone!" she demanded just as he answered. "It's your sister. Are you awake?"

"I am now," he answered sleepily. "What's up? It's almost dawn. Jesus. He didn't hit you again, did he?"

"Not physically. Dawn?! Where are you?"

"Paris. Remember?

"Sorry. It slipped my mind."

"Don't sweat it. I have to get up now anyway."

She launched into a monologue that tattled on how many drinks she had had. It wasn't the first time she had called in such a state.

"Why do you do this to yourself, Happy?" He didn't wait for her reply. "The only person Elwood Day cares about is Elwood Day. He treats you like crap. He's done this before, and as you know, he will do it again."

"I didn't even tell you what he did, so…"

"You're too isolated. Get out of that place, get some friends."

"I have friends!" she blurted out. Tristan didn't want to stay on the line, but he also didn't want to abandon her. They hung in silence for a whole minute before he urged her to, "Say something!"

"Julie, in London."

"Oh bloody bleeding Hell. Is that right?" Tristan said in a

mock British accent which lightened her mood.

For the umpteenth time, she promised him, she would try to make some changes. It was as if their conversation had been stored in the telephone wires and when they were connected it played automatically and as effectively as elevator music.

IV

Elwood didn't return to the Ponderosa Palace but to the Denver apartment, and he continued to travel back and forth to Europe. Postcards arrived from London and Paris. He checked in electronically. Neither mentioned their estrangement or Julie for whom Happy felt both envy and gratitude. While she was getting the best of El's attention and charm, she was also keeping him occupied, so Happy could lose herself in her work. Her social circle had been reduced to gallery owners, fundraisers and socialites for whom an accomplished artist was an attractive addition at soirées; although, she rarely attended. She preferred the worlds she created on her canvases.

Mornings she fortified her breakfast of protein pills which she swallowed down vodka, a splash of apricot nectar and one of lime juice for vitamin C. She showered, slipped on her silk outfit and ran her hand over the gold and silver beauty cream jars in the same manner that she held it over her palette before choosing a color. She settled on a large jar full of, her favorite mask. To the sounds of classical guitar, she slathered on a generous layer of the cobalt blue glop. She held her chin up so it would not drip. Swirling a dollop of red on her palette, she paused to remove her ring and heard a loud crash. It sounded like a terracotta pot breaking on the terrace.

Footsteps coming from the room that El called, "his home office," though he never once used it, led her to think he may have spent the night in a guest room and slipped quietly passed her. "El!" she sang out cheerfully from her studio which was a good distance away, but he was not there; a stranger was, a young man. Her bare feet on the rugs had not alerted him to her arrival. His faded plaid shirt hung loosely over his dark, sinewy arms and broad shoulders while he rummaged tenuously through the desk. She checked for a weapon and saw none. Knowledge that the silent alarm must have gone off at the security agency, allowed her to feel safe and speak coolly. "Did you lose something?" Startled, he jumped and raised his eyes to her blue-glop mask. He yelped, retreated to the high corner window through which he had entered and considered leaving but it was beyond his reach it. He paced to and fro in the tiny space like a trapped animal. With her foot, she shoved the wheeled office chair to him.

"Would this help?"

He wiped his nose on the back of his hand, sniffed, popped his tattered collar then shoved his hands in his pockets. Swaying slightly, she held up the remains of the vodka bottle.

"If you're not leaving then how about a drink?" she asked trying not to crack the mask.

"Qué? What?" he asked confused by the request.

"Drink?" she repeated and sloshed the bottle. "I bet you could use one." The house phone rang, and she held up her index finger and lifted the receiver. "Yes, everything's fine," she slurred slightly and covered the mouthpiece. "You're not going to hurt me, are you?"

He shook his unkempt mop of thick, shaggy, black hair.

"I forgot to turn the alarm off when I got up. Thank you." When she placed the receiver in its cradle, pieces of the clay mask crumbled off. "Don't get any ideas. I have a gun," she warned him softly.

"A gun! Don' shoot me!" he gushed passionately, and hung his head, "I looking for the money. Lociento. Sorry."

"Did you want a drink or not?"

Puzzled and frightened by her unexpected behavior, he wrung his hands.

"If you don't want a drink fine, but please don't leave through the window. The gardener was just here," she explained.

Happy, though quite inebriated, was keenly aware that the intruder was on her heels, so she headed to the kitchen where the large sliding doors provided the easiest exit. He leaned tentatively at the door while she washed the mask off, grabbed up a towel and patted her skin. She dropped the towel on the counter and he gasped. "Ayee. Lindo. Tú es muy lindo seniorita," he exclaimed softly and ogled her long eyelashes outlining her light hazel eyes in black.

"I am seniōra, she said showing him her wedding ring," and I'm Happy."

She pulled her lipstick from her pocket and daubed the lush crème on her mouth, poured two drinks and slid one across the table to him. In one swift gesture, he picked it up, chugged it and slid it back. Assuming he wanted a refill, she gave him one.

"Gracias."

"I am Happy, the unhappy artist," she defined further with her voice trailing off.

Snatching up the bottle, she gestured for him to follow her. Walking behind her, he tried and failed to avert his gaze from the sensual movement of her round flesh beneath her silk pants. Happy showed him her canvases with an unsteady wave of the bottle while he tagged quietly along. Twice he stepped gingerly toward a canvas to scrutinize her strokes. With his nose inches away, he inhaled and reeled back. His sensual reaction to her art sent an unexpected twinge of excitement to the apex of her inner thighs, so she was glad curiosity lured him to her personal gallery in the next room. When he returned, pride and a sense of connectedness smacked the flats of his palms against his chest.

"Soy también un pintor, the murals," he beamed, "I paint on the building, understand? He spread his hands over the wall. "Murals. You understand?"

"I do," she smiled.

From his wallet, he pulled a few well-worn photos of his work.

"They are incredible."

"Gracias. Acrylic, for the environment."

"And they survive the elements?"

He nodded and presented another photo from his pocket. "Armando, my son and Graciela my…"

"Girlfriend?" she offered.

"More." He snapped his fingers. "Mi novia."

"Fiancée? You are going to marry her?"

"Si so I was so glad when the Senior Smith, he say he will give me mucho denero to paint one mural for him."

After a ping-pong of questions and answers, she pieced his story together. In Mexico, Mr. Smith, a visiting business man was so impressed with his work that he hired him to adorn the side of his barn and financed the journey. He finished the work, but before Mr. Smith paid for it, he fell very ill.

He nodded and added, "The housekeeper say me, the ambulance took him."

"And they didn't bring him back? Well didn't anyone else know about the arrangement?"

He shook his head. "I waited and waited. I want to go home. He did not return. Can you believe it?"

"Unfortunately, I can. So you became a bandito?"

"No. If I found money, I send it back when I am home in Mexico."

Sincerity and innocence shined in his smooth, young, tanned face and aroused her sympathy but did not completely squelch her suspicion of him. He did seem quite harmless and didn't push her to give him anything. so she chose to believe him and poured two more drinks.

"Well things do have a way of changing."

She sat at a canvas and gave a liquor fueled biography of herself, her former life in New York, her many creative friends and how everything had changed when she moved to Ponderosa with her Elwood.

"So he no love you."

"What?" she asked surprised by his remark.

Whether or not El loved her was not among the aspects of her relationship with El she had considered.

"You do much for him; give your life, your New York. Where is he?"

"Work."

"Where are the photos?" He hit the breast pocket where he kept the photo of his novia and son, "My love is here by my heart."

"Where indeed?" she replied noting that Elwood was conspicuously absent from the many photographs of her and her family.

She replenished their drinks and clicked the remote which filled the room with Spanish guitar music. It brought him to his feet with such enthusiastic spontaneity that his chair fell over.

"Ay," he hollered, downing his drink.

He stretched his arms into the air, poised his black-haired head and stomped his feet in a fiery imitation of Spanish dance. Watching his long, powerful legs absorbing the shock of his boots rejuvenated her earlier tipsy cheer. His passion was contagious. Instantly infected with the rhythmic fever, she joined him. Around and around he went in controlled sensual movements. He clapped his hands on high while inches away from him, she executed what she imagined the sharp movements of a flamenco dancer draped in a shawl.

"Bueno!" he complimented, encouraging her, admiring her, "Eso!"

He danced to the other side of the room and leaned against the wall watching her interpretation. When she stopped, he approached her with the crotch-forward gate of a seductive bar room dancer. Their mutual carnal attraction, infused with vodka, formed an energy field between them and pulled them closer and closer with every step they took until the only thing between them was the vapors of their bodies commingling in the air. He let his arms drop around her. They paused and caught their breath. His hands were on the small of her back. Her head rested comfortably against his chest and her hair tickled his chin.

"Me gusta Estados Unidos!" he declared.

"Big houses to rob," she quipped.

As soon as the words were out of her mouth, she regretted saying them.

Hurt, he pushed her away with a force that threw her off balance.

"No. No. No. Why? Why, you want to say me that?" he asked and staggered to the sink. "I need water."

"I didn't mean that. Let's dance."

Her face glowed. She clicked the song back on and flung the empty bottle down on the counter. It shattered into a thousand shimmering shards, but she left it and went after her partner. Too many drinks, too quickly had stoked her merriment but doused his bravado, and he lay sprawled along the counter with the faucet running. Above the blaring music, she commanded.

"Get up! I want to dance. Come on! Dance."

She tottered on her feet, held his limp hand and made him her unwilling partner. "Eso!" she whooped and pranced. She lifted his arm, twirled in a drunken spin, stumbled and slipped. Her arm landed on the counter. He shook his head as if he were a fighter trying to overcome a blow to the head. To steady himself, he held her and rocked back and forth. The music came to an end, but the music played on in Happy's head. She put her feet on top of his as if she were a young girl at a wedding. He hummed a tune.

"I like too much your hair." He took her hand to kiss it, but winced when he saw the sobering sight of a piece of glass sticking out of her forearm. "Aye yai yai! No. Mira!"

The booze numbed her to the pain. On the counter, there was more blood near the fragments of the broken vodka bottle. Holding her arm, he freed the large triangle of glass and her blood spurted out.

"Damn you Elwood!" Happy cursed.

"Arcangelo. Mi nombre is Arcangelo," he told her and ripped a dishtowel into strips for a tourniquet. Happy was hyperventilating. He dialed 911.

"We need one ambulance at 9735 Ponderosa Drive," he told said into the speaker while applying pressure with one hand and with the other pouring vodka into two glasses. "See? It's not so bad."

Her head fell onto his shoulder, and she downed her drink but suggested, "We better have some coffee"

"Si? Yes," he agreed enthusiastically.

As she nodded, her hair rubbed up and down against his neck. In one big movement, he simultaneously got up and seated her on the hard chair. He knelt down in front of her and put the compress on her arm. The bleeding subsided, but he tied the bandage in place.

"What is your name?"

"I told you, Happy."

"No. Your nombre."

"My nombre is Happy," she said very slowly and added, "and you are Arcangelo."

"Oh, you mean like Felicita. That's a great name." In a flash of vanity, he checked his appearance in the big, shiny, chrome coffee maker, and then said, "Bueno, Arcangelo must go, the ambulance is going to bring the police."

"No worries. I didn't call them for you. You called them for me."

He nodded in understanding and decided to make coffee, but when he opened the cupboard above the machine, he only saw liquor bottles. Happy hopped up and grabbed one with the hand of her wounded arm.

"The coffee is in there," and eyed her arm. With artistic intensity he observed her bathed in the sunlight as it illuminated her firm, martini-glass breasts. They rose and fell with her breath under her fluid camisole and delivered a soft pang of lust in him.

"No Arcangelo," he said loudly, smacked himself in the fore-head, downed the shot and hers advising, "You? No more drinks. Okay? Bueno."

Coffees in hand, they engaged in the incoherent garble that passes for conversation among those who have drunk too well. They compared the cities they had visited, but when she got to Guanajuato, he leapt up and exploded in a happy dance.

"Aye yai yai! Yes? Guanajuato? Guanajuato is my city! The same like Diego Rivera."

"I got these there," she announced matter-of-factly and tossed a handful of gleaming silver baubles on the counter..

"We have a lot of silver in my country. A lot!"

"I know. I love Mexico.

"In Guanajuato, you saw the statue of Rivera?"

Happy nodded.

"La Basilica?"

Resisting temptation sent him pacing, and he rubbed his thighs. Feeling himself in the cross hairs of her gaze, he looked for the door.

"Gracias. En verdad, desde mi corazón, porque el vodka...et, et..." Her silk gliding over her body interfered with his ability to think clearly. "Y el café, y..."

"You are a very sweet guy. I bet everyone tells you that."

She dropped to her knees in front of him.

"Felicita wait. What are you doing? I..."

With so much liquor pulsing through her, his resistance felt like rejection and snapped her out of her instinctive mode. She raised herself up and ordered him to "Get out!"

Arcangelo was stunned. "¿Qué?"

"Get out!" she shrieked.

"Felicita? What happened?" he asked softly moving toward her with a smile.

"Get out! Get out! Get out!"

Her scream burst his spell as well and sent him scrambling to the door in a bolt of panic. He ran right by Elwood and two policemen.

"Happy! Happy! What the Hell is going on?"

The police ran after Arcangelo.

Elwood grabbed her by the arms and dragged her out under the Ponderosa pines where he forced her firmly into a patio chair and glared at her.

"The security company called and...?" He moved closer to to

lower his voice while she inhaled deeply to compose herself. She stared into the distance. "God damn it! Are you listening to me? I was in a meeting…"

He hauled off and slapped her. She was too numb to feel it but his hand left a deep, red imprint.

"Jesus Happy, 'm sorry…I…"

Her alcohol thick tongue released her words slowly and softly. "Why are you her and not in Denver, or London?"

"For Christ's sakes, pull yourself together. Look at your arm!"

She rose on wobbly legs, balanced herself with her fingertips on the table and looked him right in the eyes.

"And how is Julie?"

Inconvenience and embarrassment bubbled into a foaming rage that wrapped his fingers around her neck. He squeezed so tightly, the canopy of pines reaching up to the expansive blue sky swirled and began fade. In the distance, she heard a siren blaring up the drive. Elwood felt her heart thumping in her veins, so he released his grasp. She collapsed into a chair, and he wiped his hand on his jacket.

"You didn't answer my question El."

Straightening his tie, he stepped aside so the EMT's could tend to Happy. His phone rang and in stepping in for privacy, let the long, white curtains lap outside. The medical team wanted to take her to the hospital for a "couple of stitches and a tetanus shot." She refused and insisted she was "all right." The police brought Arcangelo to her in cuffs. The welt on her face made him wince.

"Look! Look what he did to her!"

One of the officers shoved Arcangelo roughly, and with fear in his eyes, he implored her to "Tell them! Tell them I didn't do nothing, favor Seniōra Felicita."

"Who the Hell is Felicita?" Elwood demanded.

"Mrs. Day, you want to press charges?"

She focused on a spot on the floor for so long that Elwood answered for her.

"Of course she does. Tell them!" Elwood said and glared at Arcangelo. "Who are you? And what are you doing here?"

"Your job… I take care of your wife," he smirked

"Who do you think you're talking to…I ought to…"

Ma'am?" the officer asked as he positioned himself between Elwood and Arcangelo.

Ponderosa was a small town. She knew that news of the injury to her arm and the bruises on her neck would be fed into the web of local gossip as soon as the ambulance arrived, and the incident would wind up in the Ponderosa police blotter. Rubbing her neck to soothe the sting of Elwood's chokehold, she collected herself. Even though Arcangelo had broken into the house, he hadn't taken anything. She had invited him to stay, so she felt she was responsible for the whole mess.

"Happy say something! I don't have all God damn day,"

"Officer, if I file charges against my husband, can you take him?"

"Husband? What?" the officer asked scratching his head.

She lowered her hand and turned her head toward the officer to give him a clear view of Elwood's hand mark.

"She's drunk! Don't listen to her," Elwood declared in a panic, stormed to his car and plugged in to his devices.

The officer gestured to his partner to stay with him and turned to Arcangelo. "Got any identification."

Fear tensed his eyes as the officer patted his pockets. Remembering he had tossed his wallet on the table, Happy gestured for them to wait and hustled to her studio. While retrieving it, the card fell out. He was only twenty-two. She grabbed several fifties from the emergency cash she stashed in her art box and tucked them inside.

Handing it to the officer, she said, "He must have dropped it when we were dancing."

"Dancing?!" the officer echoed, glanced from Happy to Arcangelo and kept his thoughts to himself. Satisfied with the contents of the wallet, he uncuffed him. "What do you want to do about your husband, Mr. Day? You wanna file a complaint?"

"No."

"You sure?"

When she nodded, he signaled to the other officer that Elwood was free to leave. He drove off without looking back.

"Listen officer I was going to drive Arcangelo back to town,
but well…"she held up her bandaged arm.

"Don't worry. We'll take him. Where are you going amigo?" he
asked and handed him his wallet.

Checking for the photos, Arcangelo saw the money and
gratitude beamed across his face in a smile as wide as the Rio

Grande. He mouthed, "Gracias. I pay you back," to her and to the officer announced, "The bus station," loudly and clearly.

"Don't send me anything but a photograph of your art...and..." she searched for a word, "la boda."

He took her fingers in his and said, "No photos, an invitation to the wedding. Gracias. Gracias. Was a happy day for me."

"I hope you have time to buy something for Armando.".

His eyes shined brightly, "Por cierto. There is a lot between here and Guanajuato."

The officer scanned the mountains and inhaled deeply.

"Ponderosa. What a view."

His partner whistled the theme song to the TV show *Bonanza*, and he burst out laughing before he joined in. The house phone rang and rang and rang, and when it stopped, Happy's cell rang in her pocket. Elwood's image and number flashed on the front. She turned it off and watched the car careen over the rocky road winding through the panorama of the Ponderosa until it became a small puff of dust.

Through
the
Latticework

~~~

𝕾𝖆𝖓𝖈𝖙𝖚𝖘 𝕯𝖊𝖚𝖘, 𝕾𝖆𝖓𝖈𝖙𝖚𝖘 𝕱𝖔𝖗𝖙𝖎𝖘, 𝕾𝖆𝖓𝖈𝖙𝖚𝖘 𝕴𝖒𝖒𝖔𝖗𝖙𝖆𝖑𝖎𝖘, 𝖒𝖎𝖘𝖊𝖗𝖊𝖗𝖊 𝖓𝖔𝖇𝖎𝖘. 𝕲𝖑𝖔𝖗𝖎𝖆 𝕻𝖆𝖙𝖗𝖎 𝖊𝖙 𝕱𝖎𝖑𝖎𝖔 𝖊𝖙 𝕾𝖕𝖎𝖗𝖎𝖙𝖚𝖎 𝕾𝖆𝖓𝖈- 𝖙𝖔, 𝖊𝖙 𝖓𝖚𝖓𝖈 𝖊𝖙 𝖘𝖊𝖒𝖕𝖊𝖗, 𝖊𝖙 𝖎𝖓 𝖘𝖆𝖊𝖈𝖚𝖑𝖆 𝖘𝖆𝖊𝖈𝖚𝖑𝖔𝖗𝖚𝖒. 𝕬𝖒𝖊𝖓.[1]

---

[1] Holy God, Holy Mighty, Holy Immortal One, have mercy on us. Glory to the Father and the Son and the Holy Spirit, and now and ever, and in the ever and ever. Amen.

Through the Latticework

The ancient father always cast his eyes downward when he crept passed the mirror hanging on the wall leading to the sanctuary. Old age had shrunk his skeleton, so the only way he was able to adjust his eyeglasses was to rise up on tip-toe, a habit that was an unhappy reminder he was no longer the tall muscular man he once was. A few years ago, the skyscraper being built across the street further reduced his stature when its incredible weight sank the church a few inches. The company that owned the building freely opened its coffers to "do whatever necessary" to prevent the historic church from crumbing into rubble, "And turning me into a very short, old man," the father joked. After three hundred years of life, the mighty granite and gneiss stone walls were buckling inward, and a restoration company was brought in for repairs which the claimed amounted to deconstructing and re-constructing them. This required the removal of a large portion of the roof. A crane lowered the foreman and a crew member in by the dome, so they could stand on the incredibly high upper boards of the scaffolding.

"They sure coulda used a crane at Copernicus."

"Sounds familiar. Where is it again?" the crewman asked.

"Where a bunch of Christ's followers busted through the roof and dropped a paralyzed guy in, so he could heal him."

"Oh yeah. I remember," he said smacking his head. "Christ was such a rock star… So that was at Copperknickers?"

Incredulous at how far from the correct name of the city the man had gone, the father shook his head and stifled a laugh.

"Copperknickers must be where they got the idea for that copper underwear? My brother…"

"Stop it! Stop it!" bellowed the project manager in utter frustration from on high. He bent over the opening and ticked off his points on his fingers. "Copper Knickers is not a place. Copernicus is an astronomer, and the place where Christ healed the paralyzed guy is Capernaum."

Such were the work crew's conversations that amused the father each day while he sat both reading and eavesdropping. He was a little sad when, in order for the stone masons to address the wall, the roofers took temporary leave. Before they did, they moved various religious objects out of harm's way. The foreman belied his crude manners and carefully held a mirror in a gilded frame in his large, work-knotted hands. "What a beautiful thing. And think of all the guilty faces heading to confession it has seen. Wouldn't want it to go missing, turn up with one of those thieving masons in an antique shop." The roofers guffawed boisterously over the jab. "Let's make sure it's here when we come back." They threw a very thick rope around a rafter far from the wall where it would be safe.

With the mirror on high, it no longer reflected the ancient priest's deteriorating physique but a view of nature's ever-changing vistas; glorious sunny days; dark, menacing rain clouds; summer evenings of blinking fireflies, colorful sunsets or a flock of birds which came daily. As he shuffled and waddled into the church, he deliberately paused to observe them. The closer they came, the larger they grew. Today, he threw his arm up and then ducked to dodge them as they zoomed into the nave. They were so fast, he expected a hawk was in pursuit, but one did not arrive. In unison, the birds blasted in and then out, except for one that was white as snow but for a small grey feathered heart between its eyes. It dived to the floor and under the pew in a flurry of down. The father wiped his glasses and put them back on to check for the little bird that seemed to have suffered a serious crash landing, but in the very place he expected it to be there was a small, thin, wispy-haired girl, who he guessed was about seven or eight.

"What are you doing there?"

"Me? Nothing," she said nervously. "Just...um," she shrugged and backed toward the seat where her pocket book and rosary lay. With a wave of his hand, the father stemmed any explanation and asked himself, *Why is it so difficult for the young to simply say 'My mother made me come,' or 'I am here to confess, to save my soul' or 'receive the Virgin Mary's promises?' Why must they always concoct a story?* Sighing heavily, he glanced around the otherwise empty church. *One little child?* he remarked outloud to himself. *Once upon a time, there were lines for confession and...* He interrupted himself to ask her "Did you see a bird back there, a little white one?" She shook her head. "Have you seen anyone else?" She pointed to the little red orb glowing above the confessional. The stern manner in which he glared at her dropped her head in prayer.

In the dank confessional chamber, the penitent stimulating the light waited patiently for the priest to slide back the partition. She wished he would hurry, for the small, enclosed compartment made her feel claustrophobic, and the longer she faced the walls' vertical wooden planks, the more she thought it resembled a coffin on end. Her soft, silk skirt bunched uncomfortably beneath her knees, so she folded her shawl and placed it under them. The act of rising turned off the red light. Though the child in the

31

nave was spinning herself dizzy, she stopped when the light went off and scrambled to her belongings. After straightening her clothes, she faced front. Not only was the light again on but the father had come back out to pick up a small paper bag he had dropped.

While reinstalling his pontifical weight into place in the compartment, he reviewed his pre-dawn reading: the homily for Sunday; his grocery list that included a block of "Stinking Bishop" cheese if it really existed; Ovid's story of the mythological Greek hunting gods Actaeon and Artemis and a question in the "Letters to the Editor" section of the newspaper. "In the course of a priest's service, how many confessions does he hear?" *Innumerabilia,* he thought but guestimated the number of confessions he had heard over the decades to be somewhere around a half a million. Penitents had once eagerly, reluctantly, angrily and matter-of-factly unburdened their sins: pleasuring themselves; cheating on their spouses, mentally and physically, contemplating murdering their exes, neighbors, in-laws and spouses, stealing objects meaningless and treasured; consenting to euthanasia for a parent or encouraging a daughter to terminate the life she carried. On the one hand, his duties of alleviating their shame and reuniting them with Christ brought him unforeseen satisfaction but on the other hand they challenged him.

Born to privilege, he had thoroughly enjoyed its attendant entitlement and popularity, however superficial, but he was called to Christ which was not the great mystery his friends and family thought, but an epiphany upon his umpteenth reading of the Gospel of Mathew. "If you want to be perfect, go, sell your possessions and give to the poor, and you will have treasure in heaven. Then come, follow me." Although, at times, he was certain he would not be able to endure the oath of poverty, obedience and chastity, especially the latter because his classic handsomeness lured a brilliant constellation of comely women to him, and he was forever confessing to how much he reveled in their adoration and fantasies he had about them. Neither devotion nor cold showers were antidotes for his primitive urges. Thus, he chose the free-flowing cassock over trousers to address the congregation. It included young ladies in short dresses who were careless about how they sat, unwittingly and deliberately, presenting him with stimulating front pew views. How priests managed to control themselves in the days before the confessional partition became de rigueur and penitents had to kneel right in front of them, bewildered him. *Those priests must have been aroused by masturbators and adulterers deeds recounted in graphic detail?* He tempered overly descriptive confessions by reminding penitents, "The basics will do," and over time, he transcended most of his involuntary responses. His spirit had melded with his commitment to Christ and rendered tales and imaginings of sexual escapades innocuous except when the penitent was Beata, lovely virginal Beata. When he heard her mellifluous voice, he would peek in to see her big brown eyes flashing innocently as she confessed the tiniest of infractions, having thought badly of someone or telling a fib to her parents. Lust would trickle perspiration down his brow and crack his voice when he consoled her. "Worry not. Your covenant with God is still intact. However, it is good you came to confession, for small sins do have a way of leading one, little by little to mortal sins. We humans were cast out of the Kingdom of God for the simple reason that we are weak. Being a sinner and practicing falsehoods, idolizing false gods... fornicating..." he stopped. Previously he had eliminated that word because it elicited tittering among adolescents and immature adults, but he was using all the words he had to hold her there a little while longer.

Once he had inserted himself into his compartment, he engaged in the pleasure of his simple routine. He whisked away the coating of dust, increased by construction, checked for spiders and then arranged his priestly panoply of necessities to see him through his hours of sitting: hard candies nestled on the shelf next to a bottle of water; the fluffed pillow under his duff; a handkerchief tucked up his sleeve and a flask of whisky slipped in his pocket. He was ready, but just as he was about to access the latticework, images from Ovid's tale invaded his calm, and then flickered before his eyes like a zoetrope. Experience had proven the best way to be rid of stubborn musings was to indulge them, and so he did.

Artemis bathing in the secluded grotto streamed into sight as "chaste and stunning to behold," as the book had described her. Around her was her lush coterie of wood nymph handmaidens, whose ruthless beauty, some admirers claimed, far surpassed the goddess'. With expertise and care, they coiffed her hair and tended to her sumptuous, milky-white flesh. Happening upon the sensual scene was Actaeon who had become separated from his companions and hunting dogs. His Eyes devoured the gifts that nature had bestowed upon Artemis, generous, round breasts and long, graceful thighs. Upon becoming aware of Actaeon's presence, the nymphs squealed in shy alarm, but Artemis, grew furious that Actaeon had dared to feast so ravenously upon her nudity that had been protected from men since birth. She demanded he not speak, but when his fellow huntsmen, who were searching for him, called out; he automatically responded. Artemis splashed Actaeon with the grotto waters which, unbeknownst to him, had magical transformative powers. As he ran back to his friends, antlers sprouted from his ears, fur covered his face, and he became a buck. The change was so complete, his own hounds, having failed to recognize him, savagely brought him down as Actaeon had trained them to do. He cried out for the dogs to stop, but thanks to Artemis' witchcraft, all they heard were the usual ghastly sounds of an animal being shredded into a bloody carcass. When the gruesome sight came into view, the father's vision ended. He shook any remnants from his head, took a long, deep breath and at last, slid aside the partition covering the latticework.

As he often did, he played a little game with himself to guess the age and gender of the penitent. The scent of wild lilacs told him a woman was there, perhaps in her thirties or forties because over the years, he had occasion to see the penitents in passing as they exited. Those much younger or older did not usually wear heady florals which was presently so strong he imagined the woman had recently daubed it behind her ears or on her wrists. The compartments were always incredibly warm in summer, and fragrances lingered in the humidity and rendered him lightheaded. While he sipped water, her enchanting voice floated through. "Bless me Father for I have sinned..." The little girl in the nave had resumed her spinning which brought her close to front of the confessional. Rather than retreat, she mischievously leaned forward to better hear. "I believe in God, the Father Almighty, Creator of Heaven and earth; and in Jesus Christ," but then she heard, "His only Son, our Lord who was conceived by the Holy Spirit, born of the Virgin Mary, suffered under Pontius Pilate, was crucified, died, and was buried. He descended into hell; the…"

The little girl wondered, *Am I supposed to know that last part?* and quickly soft-shoed back to her seat to decide which of her bad deeds truly constituted sins. *Stealing chocolate from my little brother? That is a sin. And that day I told mother I was late because the teacher kept me. She did not. I lied to my mother, but it is such a small one. I was playing with that little doggie, Max. Maybe that is not a sin? I did say 'God damn it', but not to take the Lord's name in vain. Stupid Johnny McIntyre said I'd fall down dead if I said it.* Rethinking the last two, she scanned the ceiling. The white dove fluttered slowly hither and thither around the nave and alighted, first on the statue of a saint, then on another, the Virgin Mary and finally atop Christ's head. She gasped and tiptoed to the altar to let the bird know it was "gonna get in trouble," and she scooted him away as quietly as she could. Once Christ was no longer in danger of being befouled, she plunked herself contentedly in the pew.

Inside the confessional, the scented penitent admitted hesitantly, "It's been at least a century since my last confession," and the father chuckled at her exaggeration. Her long, dark, auburn locks penetrated the spaces in the latticework. One ringlet brushed across the back of his hand, tempting him to feel it, but he resisted.

"I see. One should try to confess as soon after committing a sin as soon as possible, so…"

"I know, but a long time ago… I renounced the church."

"But you can not renounce the church."

"Your baptism created the sacramental bond of your belonging to this church, to the Body of Christ. It is as impossible to reject that as it is to reject your soul."

"I pray you are right. My life is almost over."

The ominous revelation from a penitent who whose tone was

vivacious and lovely aroused his curiosity and encouraged him to do something he had never before done; he lowered his head and peered deliberately inside. A shaft of light penetrated the lilac scent and illuminated her rhinestone crucifix twinkled wondrously on her fragile blouse sliding over her bosom as she breathed, and he paid such close attention that he began to inhale and exhale with her, and that made his breathing audible. He hushed himself by pressing his lips together and placing his hand on his chest which knocked his ring against the shelf and startled them both. Though he jerked himself away unseen, he had caught a glimpse of her great, dark, glinty eyes and delicately symmetrical countenance. She was, as he surmised, quite young but also, to his utter amazement, a veritable reincarnation of Beata. He leaned back against the wall. *She looks just like her, at least as I remember her.* Realizing how foolish the idea was, he shook it out of his head. *She would have to be as old and decrepit as I am now.*

"When you say your life is almost over, it sounds as if you are dying?" he told her.

"Experts say I am already dead."

"Experts?"

"Yes. The Lord is punishing me for my wrongs, but… father, may we begin again?"

"As you wish."

✳✳✳

"Bless me father for I have sinned."

"The Lord be in your heart and on your lips that you may truly and humbly confess your sins in the name of the Father, of the Son and of the Holy Spirit, Amen."

"Amen," she responded, ran her hand through her mane of hair and smiled to herself. "Being here, hearing your words does comfort me. I mention my wrongs, yet you address me so gently."

"Praying not to be led into temptation does not prevent you from going. The reality of inhabiting a mortal body, my child, is that we are doomed to sin. Thus we have the sacrament of confession, so…"

"Of course father," she interrupted but then hesitated before barely audibly confessing, "I had a relationship with a …a priest."

"Wonderful. So few reach out to us. Friendship is a great gift for…"

"I mean father, we…I loved him," she whispered.

Violating the seventh commandment with a fellow member of the clergy was the last sin the father expected from her, and he was temporarily dumbfounded. The penitent recounted the affair. The lovers' spiritual connection was palpable from the moment they met. It glowed around them in a scintillating violet aura, and when they touched actual spark shot off their fingers for all to see which easily ignited a blaze of bawdy gossip in the parish. To protect their reputations, they avoided socializing in the parish or anywhere in public during the daylight hours and permitted but the Old Man in the Moon to witness their flirtatious, intellectual talks of trees, Greek mythologies and Immanuel Kant. Soon those gave way to hand holding which escalated to platonic embraces and then restraining base carnal urges until one night, the priest proposed. She didn't have to explain. He knew the story well, for had she been older, she would have been talking about him, but he let her go on uninterrupted. They had planned to elope and begin a new life in a different parish far far away. On the appointed evening, she waited and waited for her beloved by the church garden gate, but he did not come. With her heart full of rejection, she boarded the train they were to have taken together all alone.

"What an idiot I was to even think he would choose me over God."

"Christ is a formidable rival…"

"It doesn't matter now. The cancer has spread and…"

Heavy sobs wracked her body, and he mentioned the water fountain in the hall; she could not reply.

"Lord and Redeemer bless he who alone is and..."

"Excuse me, I need a moment."

He obliged by allowing his mind to wander back into the delightful diversion of the grotto with Artemis and her wood nymph handmaidens. They were as real as if they were right in front of him, not at the grotto but the nearby shore where he often strolled. Thick tresses draped their bare breasts and bottoms as they primped and washed the gloriously uncovered goddess whose face the father's mind had replaced with the penitent's. She was wearing a flowing, sky blue gown and a Bishop's mitre. Piping Plovers sang as he danced to stay in place on the hot sand and enjoy the vision. A heated conflict arose between his pure religious spirit and his libido. Wise to the pernicious nature of Artemis' waters, he scrutinized her from what he was sure was a safe distance, but she launched the pitcher at him. The power of its contents dropped him to the ground. While he lay prostrate and paralyzed, she placed her hands on his head just as the Bishop himself had on the day he was ordained, and she said, "Let us implore God the Father almighty to multiply His heavenly gifts in this servant He has chosen for the office of the priesthood. May they fulfill by His grace the office they receive by His goodness; through Christ our Lord."

The chorus of wood-nymphs said, "Amen." They encircled him, turned his body over and playfully undressed him. One by one, their faces became those of the female parishioners from the front row and those who had responded to his gentle compassionate touches with one in kind, had firmly grasped his forearm in gratitude after the service or requested a private moment in the office. They spoke softly and stood so kittenishly close that brushing against their breasts was unavoidable. A few were more presuming, stroked his shoulder or picked "a little something from his hair." As then, guilt welled in his soul because he ached to succumb to his carnal fantasies. *Ave Maria* echoed in his head. A lanky brunette knelt down and planted moist kisses on his chest that sent a visible rush of ripples through every inch of his skin that stood his hair on end. A woman with honey-brown skin and ink-black eyes placed herself against his parched lips. *Ave Maria.* Another, splattered with freckles, took him in her mouth. *Ave Maria!! Send, Lord Jesus* to me, he pleaded to no avail. Their many anonymous hands oiled him as if they were anointing him. In fun, one of the nymphs snatched the mitre, tossed it about like a ball and gamboled down the beach leaving him alone with the penitent. Seated on the sand, she admired her hair in a hand mirror where he caught a glimpse of his face reflected as it was when he was a dashing, young priest. The penitent pressed her lips lightly on his, and he was released from his paralysis. With his strength but minimally restored, he arose, and then collapsed onto the temptation of her thighs and the furry origin of the world. He prayed, "Send, Lord Jesus, the Holy Spirit, to strength-en your servant in this moment of trial that the flesh may be mastered," and suddenly, he was delivered, still dreaming, from the seaside to the sanctuary. The little snow-white dove cooed above the confessional. When he saw the penitent, illuminated by a glorious halo beside him, his heart beat a wild tattoo. *You are my Beata. How I have longed to see you again.* He moved excruciatingly slowly toward her so as not disturb the hallucination in any way.

The woman awakened to his breath on her face which she touched, and then she recognized him, or thought she had, and snatched her hand back in disbelief "Ennis? Ennis is it really you?"

"Beata?"

"Yes."

They hung in silent disbelief gazing into each other's eyes. He prayed he would never ever wake up if he was dreaming.

She turned away and continued her story.

"I didn't take the very next train. I waited for you until dawn."

"I swear by all that is holy Beata that I was flying to you on the winged feet of love when…"

"Please, don't tell me a tale. I have so little time left."

"It is the truth!" he insisted, parted his hair and revealed a wide, jagged scar in his scalp so grotesque that she winced and recoiled

"What happened?!"

"A horse and wagon, or so they say."

"Or so they say?"

"Yes, after the accident, I did not remember anything, not even who I was throughout the spring, the summer and part of the fall. Without my cassock and collar, I was the 'mystery man' in room 940."

"I had no idea. …"

"No one in the parish did. I am sorry if I hurt you Beata, I… "

"I was not hurt. I was ashamed because I had tempted you because I had not encouraged you to return to God." Ennis pulled her into his arms. "When you did not arrive, I decided to make it easier for you, and I left."

"And in returning, you answered my prayers to see you again."

"Our prayers Ennis; I wanted to see you before I die. I didn't know if you would be here."

"I am. I am here, and I will be with you, pray for you to be healed."

"It's too late."

"It's never too late."

Love's magnetism vanquished their flimsy restraint, and they kissed, lightly at first, and then deliciously passionately. With the grace of modern dancers, they reveled in each other's sensual touch for which they had ached so long. Their writhing and twisting eventually aligned their faces with their hips and continued pleasuring each other with their ardent tongues. Abruptly, he stopped and slid onto her to take her, to watch her expression change as he penetrated her. He envisioned himself a match, fervidly striking and striking and striking until it ignited, melted lust's candle and eventually left them breathlessly sated on the ground. They basked in the afterglow with interlaced fingers, but then he wept, for all those years ago, when he had come out of the coma Beata was absent from his memory. When she finally came to mind, he did not pursue her but attempted to purge her and their deeds with confession.

"Ennis, what's wrong?"

"We are no better than animals giving in to our desires like that," he all but shouted in shame.

"Do you remember what you said after the first time we kissed?" He shook his head. "'He does not expect as much of people as they expect of themselves.'"

"Come. Let us pray for your recovery and for forgiveness," he pleaded.

Beata shook her head and, with tears of adoration brimming in her eyes, said, "But Ennis, gifting ourselves to each other in love should not be a sin."

"That is not for us to decide."

He kissed her palms, placed them together and clasped his own around them. In the vast, cool awe-inspiring silence that precedes sunrise, they prayed. Their answer came from a loud soothing voice on high. "The Lord in his goodness fills you both with his blessings. That which God has joined, men must not divide." When the voice stopped, each felt in the other's hand a rush of unimaginable joy and the light of a glorious new day rose in the sky. While basking in their holy union, their souls ascended and intertwined in an aurora borealis-like display that danced in the clouds slowly and gracefully until a swell of dark grey swiftly overtook them. The air grew cold. They shivered and clung to each other for security while the church walls cracked and crumbled into dust and the very ground beneath their feet split and dropped them into an abyss.

Ennis was slumped in a heap; the latticework pressed against his nose and forehead. He peered in. He saw nothing. He wiped his glasses and looked again. There was nothing. He inhaled deeply but instead of the scent of lilacs or sea air, he got a nose full of rock dusted dampness. Bewildered, he whispered, "Beata?" several times, and then he bellowed desperately, "Beata!" and buried his face in his hands bawling out of fear of the unknown and of being alone in that dark place. Time untold passed before a light as bright as the noonday sun illuminated the space and a flurry of down fluffed in the air. The little snow-white bird with the feathered heart between its eyes chirped sweetly and whirled wildly in circles until he became the wispy-haired girl Ennis had seen in the church. Angelically, she winged but feet above him before she reached out to him. As soon as he touched her, sparks shot off their hands, and she morphed into his Beata. Wings unfurled from his shoulders and together, they rose into the air by the mirror. In it they saw themselves as a white star in the center of a pitch black universe.

***

Unnerved by the sudden quake and the anticipation of an aftershock, the roofers retuned to survey the site. They clomped cautiously amid the sacred shards and slapped the dirt from their clothes. They tiptoed over stained glass fragments, climbed over chunks of the fallen dome that had collapsed and sent stone angels and saints flying and the crucifix crashing to the mosaic floor. A husky roofer crossed himself and genuflected for a moment of contemplation before he grabbed the giant Christ firmly around his waist and painstakingly lugged him to a column where he propped him up. Outside, gnarled tree roots writhed agonizingly along side piles of stones that had been the walls. Many had tumbled into a massive fissure that the quake had opened through the length of the garden, and the broken church pipes had flooded into a river; it was dammed with a morbid stack of old waterlogged caskets. They clunked and thudded against each other with uprooted shrubs and flowers, enormous candle sticks and religious statuary, one of which the husky roofer claimed was the virgin Mary. She was face down on the latticework that covered another statue, invisible but for its fingers.

"Ha! No burial plot or cemetery on these plans," the project manager noted.

"What about the job?" the burly roofer asked scrunching his face in worry.

"I got lots of jobs for youse," the foreman replied and pointed to the rafters. "Look! Our mirror survived!"

Upon seeing it dangling securely from the rope to which they had attached it earlier, the men let out a small collective cheer. Proudly, they turned their eyes from the black mirror to the clear blue sky it should have reflected and back again.

"Spoke too soon. It's broken."

The vibration of an aftershock dropped the men to the ground with their arms over their heads. The mirror fell and smashed into smithereens. When the earth stopped shaking, the foreman ordered them to, "Get out! Everybody out!"

"What about Mary?" the burly roofer asked and entreated the others to "Help me get her out of the water." No one moved. "Come on. Just take a second."

At the edge of the fissure, the men gazed into the water in awe. The statues and the latticework were gone.

Faraway/Closeby

Sous les Laurels, Etienne Dinet 1891

Faraway/Closeby

Josephine thought her disdain for men had reached its zenith when she came home unexpectedly early one day to find Conrad, her husband, standing supporting the slim weight of a young brunette squirming herself into a frenzy over his body. Conrad was a newly appointed professor of Theoretical Chemistry, tall, young, handsome; one of the extraordinary school of scholars who exercises both mind and body. He was a cyclist, and apparently so was his paramour. Their helmets lay on top of one another, their bikes against the kitchen door leading to the garden. He always smiled proudly when he related to people.

"None of the women guessed I was the professor when I walked in the class. No one did."

Jo, as her friends called her, concluded the young woman in her kitchen, on her man to have been one of those impressed by his position and clueless about his marital status; after all, Conrad had stopped wearing his wedding ring shortly after they had gotten married. That was thirty-six months ago. She felt pity for the girl but malice for him; it swelled in her chest. His pants were mangled unattractively around his feet on the floor, and he was so engaged in bipedal passion that when he looked at Jo, he didn't see her until she shrieked.

"Conrad? What the Hell?"

He dropped the girl and startled her. Jo put her hands on her hips and introduced herself.

"Hello. I'm Professor Ligouzatte's wife. I live here. And you are?"

Clothes were snatched, pots were thrown and doors were slammed repeatedly for a long while after the girl had slipped on her tattered jeans and bolted through the garden chanting softly.

"Sorry. Sorry I didn't know."

Jo caught herself foolishly listening as Conrad tried in earnest to explain how what she had seen with her own eyes was not what she had seen. From his perspective, his obvious display of infidelity didn't exist, or if it did, it was a meaningless encounter and his "initial kitchen collusion, had not culminated in the desired results. She came on to me. Really Jo, I just invited her in for some water," he continued defensively, fumbled for the green glass bottle on the counter and held it up to show her. She could neither see it nor hear him; anger had muted the sound of his voice. There was no forgiveness left in her heart. This was the third time that she knew about anyway. Miller, Jo's closest friend, who had just broken up with a man he had met three weeks earlier, was the first to commiserate with her.

"I know. I know. I know the pain you feel. No one wants to prolong a divorce, but asking for the house is reasonable. It's partly mine after all the landscaping I did there, those lilacs that Conrad had me put in during the night so they would magically appear for you, and…"

"There are other options."

"Ha. You can't really think Conrad will go to counseling."

"He might. And houses…well, we can work property out later."

"Ah, the rich. We do have the luxury of time, don't we? Where will you go?"

"I don't know Mills, Somewhere Faraway/Closeby."

"Faraway/Closeby? I never understand what you mean by that Jo. If you don't want to tell me, then don't."

He tipped his champagne flute toward his mouth for a long sip and let his voice sigh out.

"As you know, I never cared for Conrad."

"You mean as a person. I saw how you looked at him on the beach."

"I didn't care for his personality. Appreciating his physique is another story. Someone else will come along Jo, someone better. You'll see."

Someone better never appeared, but someone else showed up repeatedly. He appeared among Jo and Conrad's mutual male friends, one after the other. One sided with Jo and sympathized his way to a dinner invitation; another thought she should have sought revenge and had sex with him. Several declared long hidden passions, and one claimed never to have noticed, "Just how beautiful your legs are." The men's behavior resembled neither friendship nor courtship but sexship: a languid dinner, a long embrace, a light stroke with a fingernail down her spine, a bit of "heart-to heart" conversation, shallow and meaningless or deep and meaningful, it all led to the inevitable bedroom-eyed offers of sensual consolation. The sweetly crafted lines poured in, but instead of fomenting desire, they fermented into an even greater disdain for men. One night she pulled herself away from the delivery of another dank, hope-filled goodnight kiss and calmly delivered an unbelievable excuse.

"I have to go. I think my house is on fire."

She ran off. Her kitten heels pattered a smooth beat on the rough brick Cambridge sidewalks. She ran as many people did in cities. They were chasing down taxis, or time or fun like the group of boisterous boys she had passed. Breezing by two men, she heard one ask the other.

"Those boys after her?"

She wanted to stop and explain to them that it was not the boisterous boys who were hunting her but the men who perceived her as a lascivious lioness that could be bagged with a fancy garden salad with dressing on the side. She didn't. She ran into her apartment and slammed the door. The small wooden sign she had painted in flowery Pennsylvania Dutch style letters reading "Faraway/Closeby" clunked lightly reminding her once again to tack it down. Comfortably enfolded in the arms of solitude, she felt safe. The phone began to ring; she pressed, "Ignore" and then powered it down. Incommunicado she remained for several days. When the walls began to close in on her, she powered it back up. As usual, Miller had left several detailed messages providing updates for his busy schedule. There were auctions, museum shows and gallery talks. Upon returning the call, she learned from his outgoing message that he was "away in New York."

Consulting November 5 in her daybook, she realized she was supposed to be at her doctor's in a couple of hours, so she leafed through the pages to see where she was expected in the near future. Appointments were inked out to just about everyone except her psychiatrist, Dr. Allen.

"Consider keeping a few of them. The holidays are here," he told her in their last session.

Socializing was impossible as far as Jo was concerned. She preferred devoting her time to coming to terms with the failing marriage. She had set aside a considerable amount of time to ponder where the relationship went wrong. Was it because she did not initially love Conrad? Had it not been for his interest in purchasing art, they never would have met because she didn't know anything about his field, theoretical chemistry. When Mills initially suspected an affair, she described Conrad as "comically clumsy, overly analytical and far too serious, someone who could only be material for friendship, not amour or marriage." Eventually, his shy, gentle, patient nature allowed her to feel good about herself and elevated him from amity to love, or something she thought was love. When he asked her to marry him, she agreed. And during the heady honeymoon phase, she was convinced they were truly in love, and she had made the right choice. When he went to conferences, she missed him, and perhaps most importantly, she trusted him. Six months ago, the revelation of his indiscretions dissipated that trust into the universe and replaced it with cynicism. Her manners and niceness hid behind a new captious demeanor. Attempts at talking to strangers resulted in words spoken in short, fierce, anger-laden bursts; she didn't seem to have any control.

People are awful, she said to herself.

Therefore, when she first saw a young woman in the doctor's office during an abnormally long wait, she ignored her and indulged in the time-honored tradition of dated-magazine-reading, but there was only one. After a second time through, she sought out of the window. Nature was at work redressing itself for winter. It was not quite 3:30, yet the grey light of late autumn faded softly from the sky. The trees rustled up their withering leaves in their branches and flung them into the wind. The large ones wafted into the distance; the small ones spun in circles on the ground. Jo thought about them for a minute and concluded love and deciduous leaves had much in common. Each one bursts into being with the promise of verdant maturation. There was no expectation of forever. Its limited life expectancy, written in its DNA, forces it to bloom and grow and wither into nothingness within a predetermined period. One leaf spun in a solitary crackling circle by itself just before being crushed under a construction worker's foot.

She had seen him somewhere before; he was unforgettable. He wore a fluorescent pink hard hat with "Spike" scrawled across the back in bold black letters. He had stepped out of the coffee shop, leaned against the building in an unwittingly, steamy stance to sip his coffee, and then walked off in exactly the same direction as he had twelve weeks ago the last time she had been to the doctor. She guessed she must have been bored and drawn to the window then as well. She scanned the streets for others who might be rotating along in the same life orbit as she. Her attention was pulled back to the room when Susan, the nurse, appeared with her contrite smile, and "an emergency procedure" as the reason for the long wait.

"Susan, what happened to all the magazines?"

"We tossed them all because one of our patient's husbands was supposed to bring a big box of newer one."

"But didn't"

"No yet. Sorry."

Jo felt conspicuously nervous and envied the tranquility of the young woman waiting across the room. *She must just be waiting for someone,* she told herself. Her head rested peacefully against a pillow and she had her feet tucked under her. An over-sized art book with a glossy cover was about to slip off her lap. It did. Josephine picked it up and returned it to her. The incredible prettiness of the young woman's face held her attention. The flawless pearl complexion and large black eyes beneath a wealth of wavy brown hair gave her the soft natural loveliness of a Pre-Raphaelite portrait. The weight of the book strained her delicate fingers. Suddenly, necessity, habit or the safe and liberating satis-faction of unburdening with a stranger caused the woman to perk up in mirthful chatter. She introduced herself as Al, "short for Allyriane," and smiled learning that Josephine shortened to Jo. She was a fourth year doctoral student in art appreciation and unexpectedly expecting. The father was a diplomat whose iden-tity she wanted to protect by withholding his name and nationality. "He's European, from a big city like Paris," was all she was willing to divulge. The rest of her story, from what Jo understood was that the father was the son of a diplomat whose family did not approve of his dating an American, a foreigner. Their sternly expressed disapproval of his choice had led him and Al into seeing one another surreptitiously. Then the baby came along, and getting rid of it was unthinkable to both. It was a sticky situation.

"What about your studies?" she asked pointing to the book.

Al ignored her and chirped on with pride predicting the beauty and brilliance of her baby.

"He is perfect, as a human, a physicist; everyone knows they have evenly developed right and left brains. That's why they are perspicacious and poetic, that's why I fell in love with him. He's great."

"Great? Oh is he really?"

Dubious, Jo shook her head from side to side. She had heard it many times before, the romantic notions of a young woman placing a man's needs above her own, deluding herself into thinking her sacrifice would be rewarded with his love. Al's prattle gnawed at Jo's nerves, but she didn't dare to offer her opinion and *probably hurt her feelings.* So she was doubly happy to see the nurse come in.

"Okay Jo. We're ready."

"Oh, she was here long before me."

"I was already seen. I'm just waiting..." she concluded by holding up her cell phone.

Jo took a few steps and then returned to the young woman and handed her one of her cards.

"If you ever wanted to come to the gallery..."

"Thank you. I'd really like to see your work."

"My work?" Jo asked.

Al's eyes landed on a patch of orange paint on the back of Jo's hand.

"You're an artist, aren't you?"

"That's what I keep telling myself," she said with a chuckle.

After her abbreviated appointment, Jo sauntered home through Harvard Square amid a flurry of autumn leaves falling around couples who were snoozling against one another at the outdoor cafes; she cringed at the sight of intimacy and told herself, *Ha Love. She thinks that's love?* The wind snatched at the upper branches of the trees and hurled a twig of leaves into her hair. She managed to disentangle it in one piece and plopped it in the miniature silver vase on the mantle. To her surprise, her place, Faraway/Closeby, her "solo" as she called it, was coming together again. Years ago she had bought it as a studio where she could paint and a pied-à-terre for late nights in town. She never imagined staying there for more than a weekend at most, especially not when their main residence was so large, but space and Conrad were not what she wanted as much as a small, place to think which she did best when painting. In the linseed-laden air she dabbed and stroked herself out of reality and into her canvases which, once finished, she lined around the walls. All of them were inspired by phenomena of atmospheric optics she had seen or photographed in various places in the world. The most recent *Sun Dogs at Twilight* cast luminescent violet hues halfway up the pale grey walls reaching fourteen feet to the ceiling. She put on her headphones. The music and the act of creation led her into the world of her canvas. There she applied her brushes to the sky and added a molten glow to the two sundogs, the bright spots of light on the horizon.

The old German wall clock ticked away the days unnoticed to her except when the alarm went off every six hours. She set it that way deliberately to interrupt her obsessive tendency to paint beyond the point of exhaustion. Experience taught her that only resulted in subsequent sessions dedicated to repainting. Her self-imposed schedule made her efforts more fruitful and allowed her to take a brisk walk for an hour each day. It usually ended with a visit to the green grocer run by the Kim's who carried everything from asparagus to tampons, inner tubes or zippers.

Today Jo needed a greeting card for her parents in San Francisco. She chose one with a smiling turkey to soften her regrets. She planned to include a note in her best calligraphy. Her father would notice the penmanship first and be please. Her mother, Love Gingras would see, "regrets" and be displeased. She had grown up in the exclusive Arrondissement de Passy section of Paris, so it took more than fancy handwriting to catch her eye. After all she had abandoned her moneyed roots to live with those, she called "real people," in the fabled Bohemian environs of the Latin Quarter. She enjoyed telling the story of how she daringly stopped wearing a girdle the day she arrived and met the man who would be her husband, but as best as Jo could gather, her temporary residence there and marrying her father were the extent of her shedding her privileged up bringing. Protocol ran through her veins. As the lady of the house, she oversaw the execution of every detail of the Gingras' soirées and insisted that the perfect food be matched with the perfect drinks and served in the perfect dishes. That they were being consumed and swilled to quell familial tensions railing in the adjacent rooms didn't concern her. "The stage is set. I gave up directing dramas a long time ago," she claimed. However she was also a lovely hostess who welcomed each and every guest and had their wishes tended to by the staff. Still Jo dreaded the holidays but this one more than usual.

The relatives were scattered from coast to coast, and by now, she was certain they all knew about her trial separation from Conrad. The family had predicted failure from the beginning, not because they considered them a poor match but because negativity was part of the family gene pool. Thus Miller who had long ago detached from his clan, almost always accompanied Jo to the ménage for moral support. Love would sing out to him as soon as he came into view.

"Ah, ma petite Tante douce."

The relationship between her mother and Miller was a mystery to her. Those who met her briefly were summed her up as "delightful," but those with intimate knowledge said she was "controlling," or "tense," as politely as possible. Miller thought she was "a hoot." With him, Jo gave an example dinner experience to her boss, Bob as a reason why she disliked going home.

"Mother calls Mills, Tante."

"Well, Tante is a wonderful old way to call me queer. It's really rather sweet. The two who crack me up are Uncle Charles and Aunt Lilly."

He imitated Uncle Charles' tight-jawed Boston accented remarks on the new car Conrad had bought.

"Oh. I heard they did poorly on crash tests."

Then he deepened his voice way down low to do Great Aunt

Lilly who had the coquettish old Grande Dame habit of placing the fingers of one hand on her chest and the back of the other on her forehead before she spoke.

"Oh you bought a house over there? Really? Over there? What a pity."

Miller concluded with his favorite conversation, from the previous Christmas. It was about Jo's childhood dog, Skylos, which had been hit by a car. Raising his hand to his head, he imitated Lilly.

"'Well of course the dog was hit. Dogs! Descendents of wolves everyone knows that. Cats are really much more civilized. I have two.'

Charles corrected her. "One. The black one died after it ate a plant," he gave a big old guffaw.

"Then they threw bread across the table at each other," Jo added.

If Joe went to Thanksgiving dinner Great Aunt Lilly was certain to be present. Married three times, divorced twice and widowed once before Uncle Charles became husband number four, she considered herself an expert on relationships. As such, she provided unsolicited advice for Jo at her wedding reception.

"Look around the room carefully dear. Your second and third husbands are probably right here. After all, courtship is the introduction, marriage the climax and divorce or death the finale."

Of late, the family had cast Jo in the role of jilted wife, though she didn't think that at all. She considered herself an iconoclastic artist who mistook lust for love with a left-brained philistine. Lost in the infatuation of their attraction, she accepted Conrad's proposal with the belief that a unified landscape of harmonious compromise would form from their two vastly divergent perspectives. She never imagined they would become two islands drifting farther and farther apart on a sea of discord. Conrad had grown up a gangling, introverted, boarding school geek ridiculed throughout his education for his stringy physique, muscular intelligence and severe myopia announced by the thickest of black-framed glasses. At some point during graduate school, he became health conscious, had laser eye surgery and began cycling. He was reborn as a handsome, athletic scholar, and that is when Josephine met him. He was an excellent conversationalist, witty and loved her art, but at twenty-eight, he could boast of very little experience with women. Jo took on the task of elevating his selfish, inexperienced, jackhammer copulating into sensual, altruistic lovemaking.

"How is your student?" Miller asked at lunch one afternoon.

"Qui docet discit"

"He who teaches learns, indeed," he sighed. "I know too well. I was very well-sought after in my salad days, and now that I am older, I am the inculcator of key virtues."

"Older? Aren't you only thirty-five or thirty-six?"

"The life expectancy in Classical Greek times was twenty-eight, and I am thirty-four, thank you."

"Lucky for you that it's the 21st century."

"Your teaching has left you positively beaming. Dare I guess there is has been an awakening?"

"I suppose it is."

With an awakening in mind and a leather-bound Kama Sutra in hand, Jo skirred off to meet Conrad where once again, they pushed and sighed and fumbled and caressed their way down the silk-carpeted lovers' lane of their rooms. To create the sensual surroundings suggested in the Kama Sutra, they had employed fragrant massage oils and colorful flower petals. Conrad refused positions which required him to stand for too long because they taxed his legs in a way that hurt when he cycled, but as a "fun experiment" he gladly attempted the Camel's Hump, the Lotus or the Rest of the Warrior. Once they sorted out who was the male and who was the female, they contorted their limbs in ways, that, based on the illustration, defied the limits of normal human anatomy and resulted more in side-aching laughter and burned backs or knees than orgasms. Only one or two positions led them to the ancient text's promise of "a phantasmagorical delirium of mystical ecstasy," and left them wordlessly spent in one another's arms.

Rapture seeking was definitely worthwhile, but it was time consuming, so they reserved PE, "pleasure experiment" as Conrad called it, for large openings in their schedules when they had little else to do. Over the first few months those appointments afforded them a better understanding of one another's bodies resulting in greater success in achieving the end goal, even on less imaginative days when they used their mundane preferences, the dresser or the stuffed chair. One lazy evening after they employed both with the added visual aid of a mirror along side the bed, Conrad asked her "stay still," because he had lost a contact. He lit a candle which cast their separate bodies as one shadow of entwined lovers. To peek under the pillow, he laid his warm torso, damp with perspiration and flower petals, onto hers and exclaimed, "Found it!" He didn't hold his contact but a sparkling, raspberry diamond ring. Sheepishly, he tried to evict the words he planned from his mouth. Instead, he put the ring on her finger, fell back on the bed and opened his arms inviting her to join him which she did. With her head against him, she heard his voice resonate deep in his chest.

"Miller told me color diamonds are…"

"You consulted Miller about this?"

"He is your best friend. So will you? Will you marry me?"

Her long silence didn't faze him. He peeled one of the rose petals they had strewn on the bed from her breast, kissed her and got lost in another thought.

"I am flattered. I think so."

He nodded and kissed her, "I hope that is a yes," he said.

What are you thinking about right now Con?"

"Whether or not rhombic type 1 proteins, nitrite reductase, pseudoazurin, and cucumber blue protein, exhibit a different structure and ESR characteristics; even though, they possess the same copper ligands as plastocyanin…"

Jo stopped listening after the words "cucumber blue."

At tea, the next day, Miller saw the ring and gasped in awe, "Oh my f-ing God, Conrad actually bought it?! I told him white diamonds are for the masses, but I never thought he would buy it. Let me explain something to you about Conrad my dear. He is a delicious hunk who adores you. The sex is almost good, and then he gives you a pink Argyle diamond. There is nothing to think about. For crying out loud, if you don't marry him, I will. Let me try it on," he insisted, slid the little ring on the tip of his pinkie and scrutinized it.

"I suppose he is the one. He's responsible, dedicated to his job, not inclined to dalliances, a nester, and he does adore me." A memory pulled her lips into a smile, but then she plunked her chin on her hand and scrunched up her face. "I don't know Mills. The evening started out romantic with candles and rose petals… making love which, by the way, is wonderful with Con, but …well…you know how I am about communication. I don't know what he is talking about half the time. How can I marry him?"

"What do you mean?"

"He was talking to me for several minutes, and I swear all I understood was 'blue cucumber' or 'cucumber blue.' How can he be the one?"

"Not the one! Not the one? You could buy a French glacier with that ring. You make him the one."

"A French glacier?"

"Yes, the Etivent family was selling one, the Gebroulaz Glacier in the Savoy province. I went to Le Rosey with one of the nephews, gorgeous, black hair, blue eyes. I still have his number. I should look him up. Are you listening Jo?"

She was not. She was with Conrad on the bed, giving him points for the manner in which he was fully present when they made love even in the most missionary way as well as his willingness to try the Kama Sutra and for consulting Mills on the ring. He was a man who did more immeasurably thoughtful things for her than any other she had known. When she expressed a preference for moving into her favorite house for the sole reason that she loved to awaken to the aroma of lilacs, he had the landscaper plant them by their bedroom window at the house he preferred the window of his overnight. To soften what she categorized as "one of the most annoying sounds," metal spoons clinking against the mugs in the morning, he purchased a little set in black lacquer ones that stirred soundlessly. Then she admired the diamond, how it captured even the tiniest raylet of light and sprayed a constellation of amorous stars everywhere, and she challenged it in the dimmest of locations.

* * *

Of course the gem twinkled as brightly three years later, in the quasi-dark under corner of the mail slot about to receive the card containing her Thanksgiving regrets. As the fairies of light flitted across the blue box, she considered the possibility that her marriage may be weakening because she had allowed madding jubilation to blind her to her instincts which had told her she should have waited to marry Conrad or not married him at all.

Loneliness sighed out of the universe and settled on her shoulders. For a brief flash she thought perhaps she should go to Thanksgiving dinner in San Francisco. Her younger brother who she adored was certain to be there. Through decades of telephone conversations, they exchanged their childhood memories, routines, fears, secrets, intimate thoughts support and advice. Amid the onslaught of critical remarks at family gatherings, each was a refuge for the other, so going wouldn't be so bad. Besides Miller had already made other plans, so not going meant ten days of solitude. She leaned on the box in contemplation a bit too quickly and sent the envelope sliding onto the other letters; thus sealing her Thanksgiving alone in New York.

At the gallery, she tried to locate the bottle of ginger wine she left there earlier. Bob was just leaving.

"Hey, Happy Turkey Jo," he called out in his big Brooklyneses accent. "Whaddya plans for the big pig-out? Headed out to the coast?"

"I don't think so."

"You know Jo, 'No man is an island,' well no woman," he added pleased with himself for his self political correction. He pointed to a small painting on the back seat of the SUV. "I'm taking that down with me. I think that'll sell better in New York. . We're eating Wednesday night. No pressure. If you wanna be with some people, I've got people. It'll be an early night. Thursday morning, Rhonda and I are driving down to the city for the parade. . . the kids..."

"That's sweet of you Bob. Thanks. I'll keep it in mind."

He jumped toward her, snatched a hug and jumped back. A long time friend, he knew he shouldn't linger too long, invade her space. He called out.

"Hey, check out the statues that guy from the South End dropped off. I'm thinking about the big one for that girl buying corporate stuff. Tell me what you think. Jo, come. Wednesday. 4:00. Lock up when you leave."

Inside, the bottle of wine was right next to the store phone which rang.

Probably someone asking about the hours, she thought.

The phone kept ringing. Prepared to break the news that they were closed, she answered.

"Galerie d'Art."

No one spoke on the other end, but she sensed someone there. Hanging in the interval of silence, the pretty face of the woman from the doctor's office came to mind.

"Al?"

"Jo?"

"Yes."

"I want to take you up on your offer."

"What? You mean now?"

While she was genuinely glad to hear from Al, she had settled into isolation mode as soon as the card had gone out to her parents. She recalled her favorite line from Wuthering Heights "a sensible man ought to find sufficient company in himself," and stored all of her social graces in a freezer in the corner of her being; she was not prepared to be company with anyone, especially not a stranger.

"So, about fifteen minutes then?" Reluctance stifled Jo's reply, and Al repeated, "Hello?"

"Well, we're closing."

"Great we'll go for coffee."

Jo suspected Al's sense of immediacy to hold a mystery and while curious, she was resigned to being alone. Al continued talking.

"It doesn't have to be any place special, someplace Faraway/Closeby would do."

Hearing her personal expression from Al thawed Jo's graces, and she smiled at the extraordinary coincidence.

"What did you say?"

"Oh it's a thing I made up, Faraway/Closeby. Someplace near that..."

"No one else knows about," they said in unison.

The phone read, "call ended," so Jo snapped it shut. It had come from a private number. She waited. No call back. Al's unexpected interruption of her life pulsed a stream of aggravation into her veins because she had already gone into the alone mode.

"Jo! Hi!"

She spun around. A mass of white November light billowed in on a zephyr and presented the sylph-like silhouette of Al. Her long fragile arms tossed a gossamer shawl in the air, and it wafted onto her head as she descended the steps into the gallery. With the simple act of mincing along the warped wooden boards into the room, she skirted passed all Joe's objections and defenses. Jo thought she was the most feminine woman she had ever seen. Watching her approach, filled her with the happiness that comes with a long–time friend, not someone she had recently met.

Al pointed out the window to the Pâtisserie Café, I have a table..."

Jo heard Dr. Allen encouraging her to open herself up to people, at least for the holidays.

"Tempting. They do have wickedly delicious profiteroles?"

Braced to tolerate a bit of pedestrian chatter on art or relationships, she sat with Al at the café, but soon found herself listening with fascination. Extensive life abroad in the exotic locals of South America and East Africa combined with Al's vast knowledge of art made her a formidable conversationalist. Fueled by two espressos, they blathered away the remainder of the café's open hours. When it closed, they relocated to a bar down the street. Their words flurried through the air and accumulated in large drifts around their table which kept the friendly, young waiters at bay.

"Your child will be because of you, not the father. Although I am not sure about your French approach to drinking while you're..."

The smile vanished from Al's face. She stared blankly into her glass of wine for a few seconds, gestured for the waiter and then glanced at her watch.

"Eleven thirty?! I haven't even unpacked." Eagerly she stood up to go.

"Unpacked?"

"Yes. They are fumigating my place."

"On your own at the holidays?"

"It happens sometimes."

Out in the night, Al discovered that her flimsy shawl was no match for November. She warmed herself by leaning into Jo, and slipping her hand into the crook of her arm. Questions about why she was staying in a hotel stayed on the tip of Jo's tongue. She didn't want to pry.

"It smells like snow or rain," Jo remarked.

"Everything smells clean after a good thunderstorm."

"Bacteria! Actinomycetes."

"What?"

"Oh silly husband trivia. Conrad knows all this stuff. The bacteria are odorless until they get wet and then the rain releases them or something. Nature's air freshener."

"Bacteria. Huh? Who knew?"

In front of the Hotel, they said good-bye with a brief embrace and a promise to call. Jo rushed back toward Harvard Square to pick up coffee milk and recapture her creative mood, but it ghosted off into the Old Burying Ground. The uneasy feeling of someone following kept her vigilant and peeking over her shoulder, but no one was there. Nothing was moving except a mass of ominous clouds. As she paused to appreciate the eloquently animated gray illumination of night stretching across the Cambridge Common, her mood croodled back into her body then flew out again. It was startled by the sudden rowdy clatter of unruly suitcase wheels and shoes banging on the bricks. Annoyed she cut her eyes in the direction of the sound to see petite Al struggling with her unwieldy luggage. With a markedly agitated air, she spoke to Jo.

"No cabs. There is not one cab at the hotel?" She propped her suitcase up and continued, "There was a mouse. A mouse! In my room... dead. Well I can't stay there."

She reached for the handle of the suitcase.

"Cabs are tough on Thanksgiving. A lot of people travel this week."

The cab stand by *the Out of Town News* kiosk in the middle of Harvard Square was empty.

"That's what they said at the hotel. They couldn't even get one on the phone for pity's sake."

The clouds melded in the sky, and a rainstorm clapped on the streets in a heavy winter rain. Al took off her strappy high-heels and grabbed one side of her suitcase while Jo grabbed the other.

"Come on; I just live across the Common."

✳✳✳

They burst into the hallway. Al stopped and let out a demure trill of laughter as she read the sign on the door, "Faraway/Closeby."

Jo pushed back the door and said, "Nous sommes chez moi, Faraway/Closeby, and put your shoes on crazy lady."

"Not really crazy," she said and held them up to reveal the name.

"I don't know if a case of pneumonia is worth a pair of shoes especially when they cost six hundred dollars."

"Seven twenty-five," Al corrected with a smile.

"As I said, 'that's crazy.'"

With a bit of cocoa, they picked up an earlier topic and parlayed it into a week long conversation. Al fit perfectly on the sectional sofa which they made up nightly, but she always ended up in Jo's room. Before turning in, Al would perch on the corner of the bed to read lines from a book or pose one last question. Eventually, to be more comfortable in continuing, she would slip under the covers and talk them to sleep.

"At least I think I went to sleep first," she told Miller.

"So now you're sleeping with this woman," he asked while arching his eyebrow.

"Sleeping. Accent on sleeping. I hardly notice her. I mean physically. Her intellect, her spirit fills the room. And she likes to read aloud, just like me."

"Up late with champagne and *The Rubyfruit Jungle*?"

"Hardly. Victorian Courtship painting. Women's intimacy is something you men, gay or not, will never get."

"Oh I forgot you have that super California king-sized bed."

"Let me tell you about the world of female heterosexuals Mills..."

"I am well-acquainted with them which is why I am so grateful I was born gay."

The chemistry and intellectual synchronicity she and Al shared was quite noticeable. They sometimes said the same thing at the same time which is what happened at Bob's the evening-before-Thanksgiving Dinner. In the roomful of strangers, Al was more animated than usual but stayed close by Jo. Miller arrived late. He complained that the train stalled coming in from Gloucester, and he had to search, "high and low for whipping cream for dessert topping." He was accompanied by a mirthless, blond hobbledehoy who he introduced as his "um cousin from out of town." They stepped out into the yard for air and Jo challenged him.

"Your cousin?"

"Well you brought a date too," he shot back and giggled.

"Al is not my date."

That night Jo and Al returned to Faraway/Closeby in an exhausted silence. The conversation they had begun days ago seemed to have finally ended. They walked in and went in separate directions, Al to the bedroom, to retrieve her bathrobe and Jo to the studio where she sat in an inebriated haze of fatigue and scanned her canvas. She called out to the guest bathroom on the way to her room.

"Al, I'm going to turn in. How about you Al?"

She realized she was not there. In the bedroom, she bumped right into her.

"Lose your way in my spacious palace?" but received no reply. "Hey, are you all right?"

Suddenly Al bent her knees and folded up on the floor. An enormous sob was suspended in her body, and she remained motionless. Jo knelt in front of her and spoke in a calm, off-handed tone.

"Whatever it is, don't expect me to tell you everything's going to be all right. I have found people say that or something like that because they really can't think of anything else to say. No one has answers to anyone else's problems, but feel free to unload if that makes you feel good."

Al dropped her head onto Jo's shoulder, slipped her arm around her waist and held onto her as if she were trying to steady herself. Hearing her sniffle, Jo gave her a tissue from her pocket.

"Should I call 911? I mean, you haven't downed eighty-three valiums, have you?" She paused and continued tenderly, "Please say you haven't." Al shook her head and suggested she relax by pulling her onto the quilt, but the gesture elicited a nervous monologue. "Well that's a relief. God I wish I had a cigarette. I never really smoked, but it was fun every now and then. I did love all the paraphernalia, golden lighters and cases," she said in one breath and then added, "If you had ever predicted I would be in bed with a woman...well I would have laughed at the very idea. Just goes to show, there are vast quantities of life beyond the limits of a person's imagination. I suppose to live a full life, we have to be open, be flexible and take chances just as we do in art. We can never tell if we have been the fool or the hero until the curtain is down and the reviews are in."

Consciously she decided to allow Al to get a word in edgewise and stopped talking, but she didn't say anything. Instead she tightened Jo's chest so she couldn't breathe by throwing one of her leg around her. The light began to blink as the bathroom bulb slowly burned out. Flickering in the dark as it did made the look like characters in an old-time movie. When the bulb died, they were immersed in invisibility. Suddenly she heard Al blow her nose and rustle around in her bag. She struck a match and lit two cigarettes. In the flame, their eyes met, and they shared a smile. Jo reached for a nearby candle, and Al clicked open a small pocket ashtray. There they lay in the loud tick of the carved German clock until a while later it chimed one.

"Your own ashtray? That's hard core."

"Toujours est préparé. Dom smokes a lot… That was very poetic."

"What?"

"Being open and flexible, not knowing anything until the reviews are in."

"Thank you. Between all that liquor and fatigue, I'm surprised anything makes sense right now. Especially drinking when you are pregnant and…smoking."

Al's cigarette jewel burned brightly when she hauled on it, "To over share for a moment…I lost the baby," Al stated in a flat tone.

"I'm so sorry. ….Do you want to talk about it?"

"That afternoon that we met in the doctor's I was almost two months along. Dom had not yet told his parents about me or the baby, but he had proposed."

Jo excused herself to round up two night caps.

"Dominique had to accompany his folks abroad, and he planned to tell them we were having a child 'when the time was right.' He sent for a family nurse to stay with me, some Mediterranean named Máygissa. I don't think she spoke English; she hardly said anything, but she was a smiling comfort, made wonderful broths and teas, but they made me worse, not better. In class, the pain was so horrific. I had to leave and go right to the hospital.

"I have heard that morning sickness can be a bitch."

"Morning sickness was not the problem. Try duplicity."

"Duplicity?"

Jo watched the conflicting urges to reveal and spill what she meant purse and twitch Al's lips for two full minutes before she opened them and let the event steam steadily out.

"The doctors wanted to know everything I had put in my mouth that week. I knew the basics but nothing about what the nurse was giving me. My neighbor has a key, so I sent her the house to ask Máygissa to make a list, or if she wasn't there, to bring the teas and bottles on the counter to the hospital. Vitamin C, capsules stuffed with parsley, dong quai, blue cohosh and..."

Jo nodded and interjected, "Prenatal..."

"Prenatal? No. Absolutely abortive in the doses she was giving me."

"A nurse gave you...!?"

"What nurse? Ha! When it was clear she wasn't returning to my apartment, I stupidly thought I would actually get her if I called Dom's, but..."

"No Máygissa."

"No one there had ever heard of her."

"How utterly diabolical and frightening," Jo said and then leaped to her feet in an empathetic and sputtering blaze. "It's reprehensible, heinous... That was his child too. What did the police say?"

Al shook her head, let out a tearful sigh of defeat, and though wounded, remained calm. "I didn't call them. I can't... I don't... You know what? I don't want to talk about it anymore Jo." Al curled up next to her in the cold room. "You don't understand."

"Understand what? Is there some greater mystery afoot?"

"I love him."

"Oh my God! I am going to pretend you didn't say that."

"Don't judge me. You still love Conrad, don't you?"

"I don't know. I had to get away from him to be able to see if his... indiscretion had destroyed that love or if it was even real in the first place. After all, love is intangible, indiscriminate, illogical and ephemeral. Studies have proven that it is a neurological condition and that the pheromones wreak havoc on our biology, our psyches. So even deep long lasting love doesn't turn out so well. Antony and Cleopatra killed themselves. Lancelot ended up a hermit and Guinevere a nun..."

"And on and on Jo, but they experienced love, true love."

The nightcap thwarted Jo's ability to construct any further quasi-intelligent points. While lying with Al, she contemplated turning up the heat, but she couldn't bring herself to leave her as she sobbed, not quite as surreptitiously as she might have thought. The sound spoke directly to Jo's heart, and enfolded her in a soothing embrace where they drifted off toward the borders of sleep. Al absent-mindedly ran her fingers over the buttons of Jo's silk pajamas. It raised a memory of her own hand when she was five-years-old.

In her mind, she saw it turn the big glass doorknob to her mother's room. She could feel of the soft cool carpet beneath her feet as she stood and strained to see her among the giant dark shadows of the room steeped in slumbering midnight. The moon's rays guided her to the bed where she climbed in and snuggled next to her mother. Fear of the boogieman or a monster hadn't sent her. She hadn't really given any thought to why the urge to be with her mother had awakened and pulled her from her bed. As she held Al's hand, she had an epiphany.

She hypothesized that she had gone to her mother because a primal form of communication had been taking place. Her mother was lying alone emitting a distress signal which she had picked up. Instinctively, she had gone to her mother not to receive comfort but to give it. Her father was rarely there. Going to that room meant going to her abandoned mother. Neither said a word. Her mother would welcome her, take her little hand in hers, kiss it and tuck it beside her. Then, together they would fall asleep as she was about to with Al.

A wave of pity for her tortured, fragile new friend washed over Jo, and she took her hand just as her mother used to take hers. *I hope I never have to meet the selfish, manipulative mur-*

ONLY HUMAN SHORT STORIES OF LOVE & LOSS...

derer who deceived her like this. Her disdain for men was fully rekindled. Al clung to her. Touching was something Jo had been without for a long time, something she needed, she wanted. They were breathing in cocktail-fueled warmth stroking each other. Al toyed with Jo's fingers and then in nudging closer feathered her hair across her face and neck. In that moment, she wanted to kiss her, really kiss her.

Suddenly, Faraway/Closeby banged with the opening and shutting of the front door. The bedroom light flicked on and Miller pranced in and looked at them with a face full of rosy mirth from beneath his hat cocked drunkenly sideways and reeking of booze. He paused long enough to run his giddy eyes over them, smirked, gazed directly at Jo and slurred out.

"Well, well, well aren't we cozy?"

"You remember Miller?" Jo asked Al who had met him earlier at the party.

He reached into the linen closet with a giggle.

"Of course she does. I am unforgettable. I just need some sheets and you can carry on with your carrying on."

Jo threw off the covers and Miller saw that both women were fully clothed.

"Lesbians are so booooooooooring."

She got a light bulb for the bathroom which Al took in with her.

"I knew you weren't going to catch the last train Mills."

Together they made the sofa bed for him while he regaled her with the details of the evening.

The next day the three of them sat down to a bleary-eyed 'hair of the dog" breakfast of Irish Coffee. A lively discussion of plans for a tropical Noel energized them.

"Ah yes," Miller said and threw his head back as if he were tossing his former full head of hair on the beach, "languishing beneath the palms, cocktails chilling in hand. I have an old flame lit on one of those beaches, maybe two. I vote for a Christmas in Bermuda."

They clunked their coffee cups together. Jo put on another pot, and thought about the impulsiveness with which they had just made plans for Christmas but thought it was just a whimsical idea. Miller tugged his hat tightly on his head, swigged the last drop and bid them adieu.

"I don't want to miss this train. Cheers."

"Sure. See you."

Al pulled papers out of her workbag and placed them in a conspicuous spot on the table before slipping out right after him. Joe breathed a sigh of relief that she was alone. The studio seemed a much brighter place since Al had been staying there. The subtle changes affected her art. Shortly after her appearance the depressing mash of dense, dark circles of black on her latest canvas exploded into vibrant swirls of glowing pastels. She begged Al's opinion; after all, she was deeply entrenched in art theory and criticism. Al always replied with a psychiatric echo.

"Well, do you like it?" she asked emphasizing "you."

Jo hated her own paintings, yet she had a difficult time parting with them. Bob liked the one with all the colors so much, he offered to hang it in the gallery in the local artists' exhibit. Leaning back, she contemplated her work and sipped her coffee. The papers Al had left on the table caught her eye. On top was an article about Étienne Dinet, a French Orientalist whose paintings of Algerian life and people they viewed recently. Jo described them as "magnificently and lavishly intimate and loving," and expressed an interest in his biography but had forgotten about it. The second was as yet untitled analyzed Jo's work. It was written in objective and positive terms by Al who had scrawled across the top, "For the catalogue of your gallery debut" used such as "masterfully executed" which she found more embarrassing than flattering.

Just as she was about to power down the phone to hide from distraction, it rang. The ID read, "Conrad." She knew he would keep calling, so she answered. He was downstairs where he had been ringing the doorbell despite the "out-of-order" sign. They had agreed to try to work things out between them. They had scheduled and cancelled several therapy appointments, so she gave in to the impromptu visit, dropped a key out of the window, mixed a pitcher of Bloody Marys and handed him a drink as soon as he walked in. Conrad appeared weathered by his new social life broadcast in several smudges of glossy pink lipstick on his collar and the scent of gin and perfume. It was only 11:30 in the morning, and he hadn't even had the decency to go home and get cleaned up before coming to see her. *The nerve* she thought. He gulped his drink and blathered on about the wild party he had attended as if he was a younger man which she thought odd because he loathed parties. A molten anger churned beneath her relatively calm surface, but when he held up his empty glass, she unceremoniously refilled it thinking, *How dare he show up like this? What is he trying to prove?*

All the aggravation of the last months of their lives together that she thought she had pushed into outer space came screaming back through the atmosphere. She sat glaring at Conrad's face. The bright, bashful look she used to cherish had been tarnished by his newfound lechery. Long nights of immoral sex and intoxicated revelry had drawn dark lines under his eyes and hollowed his cheeks. She sniffed his neck audibly.

"Geranium potluck oil. Nice, isn't it?" he asked with a crooked grin.

Under her attentive gaze, he nervously swigged his second Bloody Mary punctuating its completion with a bang of the empty glass on the table.

"Jo I was hoping, we..."

"Who are you anyway?"

"You know perfectly well who I am Jo."

"Why would I care about a party you? You know what Get out. Get out before I call the police." She flipped open her phone.

"You can't be serious," he balked.

Truly confused, he rose and shifted his weight from one foot to the other. "Out of respect, I came all the way over..."

"Respect? You fucked a girl in our kitchen?"

His jaw dropped when she swore because he had never before heard her do so.

"Our kitchen Conrad! On the God damn table we bought together."

"How could you possibly know where we...?"

"I was just guessing."

She hurled a mug at him, and he backed into the hallway. Faraway/Closeby clanked back and forth.

"What has gotten in to you? I thought..."

Next, he flung her glass, and he pulled the door shut. The drink crashed and splashed all over everything including the canvas she had stapled lightly on the wall. For a moment, there was absolute quiet. Then Conrad rapped his knuckle quickly on the door.

"Hey Jo. Faraway/Closeby. That's great. Perfect really. I like your sign."

"Go away!"

There was another knock on the door.

"Jo, could I get my coat?" he asked politely.

"It's outside."

"No I left it on the chair."

"It's outside."

He guessed she meant she was going to throw it out the window, and he scrambled down the stairs. Its tissue-soft navy cashmere arms clung to a branch where it hung upside down. The contents of his pockets rained onto the street and Conrad dashed from side to side catching his credit cards, keys, money and condoms. No matter what happened or how he felt, his voice always smoothed out in a moderate tone which annoyed her.

"Aw Jo. I think that's uncalled for. It's really a bitchy thing to do. Bitchy," he repeated under his breath.

All the while, he was jumping and taking the occasional swipe at the tree branches trying, to knock his coat free He pleaded with her to throw something heavy into the tree.

"Wait right there," she told him and observed him standing befuddled the sidewalk. *What a tragic mess he is. I should try to talk to him, but not today.* She dismissed thought and the sight of Conrad by lowering the shade. A firecracker exploded in her head and a white light blazed. It was a revelation, one of those she found in the center of a storm of anger. For a moment she hated herself for having left him, for he wasn't equipped to deal with the deliriously, toxic bacchanalian New York nights. She could see his charming boyish smile in the candlelight he arranged the night he stumbled over his proposal and then carried on about cucumber blue protein. The thought touched her heart. His honesty, innocence, caring and light-heartedness had set him apart from other men she had known and elicited unconditional trust for him. *That's it! That's why I am so pissed off! What a Pollyanna I was to think he was above betraying me.* The revelation made her want to jump out of her skin.

She donned her headphones and choked the color out of her paint tubes. Deep Sevres Blue; Sap Green and Alizarin Crimson snaked in three oozing ribbons across the treated fabric beneath a massive vein of zigzagging Titanium White. Some splattered onto the carpet and on her way to get a kitchen towel; she slipped on a blob of red which brought her tumbling into the passionate gooey rainbow. The oils under her fingertips reminded her of the flavored ones she had once used on Conrad's chest and licked off. Now in the same position over her art, she erupted in a frenzy of violent-creative energy. She tore off her clothes and slathered handfuls of paint onto her naked body. A scream escaped from her soul; she attacked the canvas with her torso and painted with her naked breasts and nipples. After awhile she stopped, leaned back on her elbows. Winter's swift night had slipped in, and she could barely see anything, not even her hand as she wiped away the oil. The strike of a match illuminated Al taping her.

"What the Hell? Turn that off! How long have you been there?"

"That was amazing," Al exclaimed. "People will be fa…"

"People?! No people. Give me the camera."

Al minced playfully into the other room. Jo went after her and tried to get the camera away, but Al fell on the bed and tucked it beneath her. Though she was quite light, Jo could not move. Al was laughing at the game-of-it all which softened Jo's mood, so she reached down and tickled her until she let out an affected trill of contagious cackling. Al slid around and danced her fingers along Jo's ribs. They were locked together in silliness. "What are you going to do now," she asked sweetly.

Al's firm body was squarely on top of Jo rhythmically sliding along her body in what felt like foreplay. Al's breasts pressed down into hers and she moaned with her eyes closed lost in the enjoyment of the contact. She hung her head and gazed dreamily into Jo's face. The idea that Al was attempting to seduce her entered and exited her mind.

"Doesn't that feel good?" Al asked grinding her bony pelvis into hers.

Not only did it feel good, it aroused her which confounded her. In rapid succession, questions flew into her head, as she tried to figure out what was happening. Was Miller right? Had Al been under the impression that their friendship was a deeper relationship all along? Had, she herself, on some level, wanted that? If a woman is excited by another woman's touch, does that mean she is a lesbian or simply that she was a sentient being? There was no time to sort out the chaos of carnal instincts versus cultural mores. She turned her full attention to Al who had unbuttoned her top and straddled her while licking her sternum. A fear-filled confusion overwhelmed her which caused her to push Al back with unintended force that sent her to the floor where she hit her head. The momentary spell was broken.

Al showered while Jo had a drink to numb the self-hatred and guilt she felt for allowing her fears to morph into the passive aggressive act. When she saw the camera on the bed, she was relieved her moment of creation would remain private. Before she took the DVD, she watched it. Everyone claimed she was a human of the mature, educated, analytical and gregarious variety, but she thought they were defining the shell that protected the real her who lived inside. That woman was so sensitive that just walking around in the world presented challenges. Watching a bee trying to fly through a window pane brought her to tears. If those around her, even total strangers were in turmoil, she felt their pain. Noises all sounded loud to her, and the sun was painfully bright; she was always upset. When Al had run her camera in the dark, she had unwittingly captured Jo's inner artist. Al had somehow come closer than anyone, even Conrad. She needed a morning cup of coffee to think, but there was no cream.

Bundled up in the square, she stopped to give a homeless woman on Mass Ave. a five dollar bill. Long ago she had stopped giving people a quarter or a dollar because coffee was so pricey. The woman insisted it was too much. When Jo finally convinced the woman to accept it, she gave her a heartfelt, mood-altering embrace. In the store, she stayed focused on the cream; otherwise, her bag would mysteriously fill up with random items which she would try once and leave in a drawer at home. The aroma of coffee welcomed her back to Faraway/Closeby.

Al dried and dressed was all smiles. "Oh great," she said when she saw the cream. "Some one lost their coat in the tree outside."

When Jo chuckled and mentioned that "Conrad forgot it when he dropped by earlier," Jo gave a quizzical look but didn't pursue the matter.

Instead, they began a dialogue which lasted through several days and bottles of wine about Al's proposal for a film to be entitled "Exorcism of a Marriage," after the painting Jo was working on when she shot it. She couldn't get it past Jo until she came up with the idea to rendered Jo unidentifiable but preserve her fascinating silhouette in the act of painting. Once finished, they showed it to Bob who thought it was "just great" and wanted to include it in the show of her paintings. The short piece was mounted in a black 3-D box next to one of the canvases and set on an infinite loop. In the dark, her bare shoulders and breasts flashed while she writhed in the primal act of creating. It was the first painting to sell. When Bob had the canvas taken down to be crated and shipped, he noticed the tiny letters written on the back. Bob read them aloud.

"Well aren't you a forgiving woman."

"Credit given where credit is due. He was the inspiration."

∗∗∗

Whether negativity should be acknowledged for creativity exchange began another extended conversation between Jo and Al. This one centered on the question, "When was cheating an unforgivable act and when was it a forgivable indiscretion?" lasted from the exhibit to the plane ride to the hotel lobby in Bermuda where they shouted above the rhythmic African Gombey Dancers. Jo thought that would be the last time, but on the beach at Aston, Al peeked out from under her red cartwheel hat and studied her face.

"I get the feeling you are not going to divorce Con."

"We are taking a break... probably like you."

"No way. "

They stood facing opposite directions on the beach stretching out before them in a white-hot coma as the relentless Bermuda sun opiated the sand.

"I thought I'd miss a white Christmas but with sand this white how can I?"

"Right."

"We always talk about me and Con. What about you and Dom? Your place must have been fumigated ten times over, yet you stayed on with me and..."

"You said you liked having me there."

I do. It's just that...well in all this time...You have never met or called, to my knowledge, to sort it out. "

"There are things you don't know."

"Right."

Al lifted her face up to Jo's and gave her a quick kiss on the lips which bumped her red hat onto the sand. Miller pranced up.

"Having fun? I am. See?" They gathered around and viewed his digital montage of beefcakes in Speedos while he commented on the attributes and flaws of each. "And what have we here?" he tittered. The final photo was a blurry shot of Al delivering her kiss to Jo. "Ah the power of the Caribbean sun to unlock inhibitions."

With adolescent glee, he took off down the beach in a flurry of gay mirth while Al dotted into the sea to retrieve her hat. "Let's belly up to the bar at 6:00!" Miller yelled at them.

They waved.

"I'll burn with no hat," Al announced shielding her face with her hands.

They decided to seek shade in a restaurant and found a place with armchairs. In a corner of the place, artists turned molten glass into a menagerie of objects, and they watched for a while. Quietly they sat and tuning into conversations near them. Every now and again, amazed by the same comment someone had made, Jo and Al would communicate with a glance of mutual understanding. With remarkable ease, they spent every waking and sleeping hour together, a thing each confessed she had never done with anyone else. They could just sit in harmonious quiet together as they did now sipping rum and reading. Jo watched as Al arose as gracefully as a whisper and tipsily wiggled her way to the ladies room. She stopped, giggled, glanced over her shoulder and steadied herself. On the brief walk over, the sun had turned her skin bright red. Jo watched her until she was out of sight. The woman next to her was complaining.

"Well I don't know what Herbert was thinking. After fourteen years of marriage, he should know better. It just isn't the sort of thing I wear. "

Jo discretely shifted in her chair to figure out what the woman was talking about. She was the taller of a pair of bejeweled maturing blondes tanned to a rich bronze. In her hands, she held an enormous hat like the one Al had lost to the water.

Her companion tried it on.

"It isn't so awful?"

The crown was too small and she lifted it off, shook out her shaggy bleached hairdo and dropped it into the shopping bag.

"Just tell him you lost it. Come on. Let's go. I thought we were shopping," she noted and clinked her ice cubes, "which I won't be able to if I have one more of these…"

"If you really don't want the hat, I'll buy it," Jo offered.

"What?" asked the woman who owned the hat.

She exchanged a glad glance with her friend who raised her eyebrows in approval. Just then, the server came by with their check.

"Okay. Pay this and it's yours."

Without looking at it, Jo took the check in one hand and the shopping bag in the other. Then the blondes turned as if they had never spoken and exited in a staccato of summer sandals and prattle.

"That is so sweet. I can't believe you did that. You bought it from her? Really? That is so sweet. Thank you," Al said when Jo presented it to her.

She hurried outside to challenge the sun with her new brim. Jo picked up the blondes' check and winced. Apparently, they had been there for sometime. It was $378.00.

There's a sucker born every minute, she said to the server and laid the women's check on hers, "and include this."

"This tab is closed already. That was a very large group and one of them made arrangements to take care of it earlier."

She accepted it as some sort of good karma, but felt guilty about getting the hat for free and tipped the server very generously. Kicking through the evening's puffy clouds and pink-grey sky reflected in the surface water on the sand, Al casually slipped her hand into the crook of Jo's arm and dropped her head against her shoulder.

"I am in the clouds in love with you."

"You're welcome, but it's just a hat."

Al took a few steps back and looked her square in the face.

"I mean it. " I love you."

Involuntarily Jo let out a nervous laugh. She felt her muscles stiffen, and the little splash of water between them spread out like the entire Caribbean. A gull let out a long hungry crying that echoed in the air. Lost under the huge brim, Al's childlike eyes beseeched Jo for a response. Then she leaned forward, pressed her body next to hers, inhaled deeply and then kissed her with passionate deliberateness. Meekly, she said one word at a time.

"I—love—you."

"You don't," Jo said firmly.

"Don't tell me what I feel?"

"If you loved me, we'd be in some room getting it on."

"Let's go," Al said without as much as a blink of her eye.

Jo unhooked Al's arm from hers and held out her arm to distance her, but Al lost her balance and staggered back into the water where she fell on her bottom. Her dress billowed around her. The sadness of rejection deepened her dark eyes. She gathered herself up and plodded crestfallen through the knee high water. The helplessness of her petite figure struggling with her hat, a shopping bag and dress, heavy with water was sad and charming. Jo was certain she would come back, but she didn't even peek over her shoulder. The urge to run after her welled up inside, but she resisted. She didn't want to deal with the emotions she was certain she would find under the cartwheel hat. So she returned to the bar and selected a bottle of Shiraz as a companion while she waited until 6:00 O'clock for Miller.

He arrived with apologies that a rendezvous with one of his suitors had escalated and not only made him late but would prevent him from staying very long.

"I didn't think you would miss me too much since you and your girlfriend," he commented peering through the camera's viewfinder, "What? Where's Al?"

"She thinks she is in love with me."

He let out a stifled howling laugh and stopped abruptly, "Oh you're serious. No!"

Jo shared the story of the hat and the declaration of love.

"And you didn't go after her?" He lowered his voice to a sympathetic tone and patted her quickly on the arm, "I understand. I understand. Difficult to be so well sought after, isn't it?" He sighed and turned his eyes toward the ceiling as he recaptured a memory. "I had a similar situation happen and with a woman. Gorgeous of course, blonde with a perfect little ski jump nose."

"Yes, yes, an heiress," Jo chided.

"As a matter of fact," Miller quipped. "She could have had anyone and she wanted me, of course I would have to convert. She took liberties with my body, sticking her hand in my shirt and rubbing my chest."

"I don't think Al is trying to convert me. Maybe transference?"

"Going down the analytical road, are we? Well the only women I have ever seen making out with each other are girls playing games, lesbians or thespians pretending to be lesbians."

"So what did you do with the heiress?"

"Proposed a marriage of convenience."

"How thoughtful."

"Yes it was. I am worth a Hell of a lot more than she was or ever will be thank you very much. I would marry me."

"Oh Mills what would I do with out you? When did you figure out you were gay?"

"Figure out? Figure out. What? I didn't. When I was four years old, I saw an Italian couple on the beach. The woman was very pretty, but I was more interested in the man in his Speedos. I couldn't take my eyes off him."

"Four? Really?"

"When did you figure out you were straight?"

"Well that's silly. I never had to ....Oh. I get it."

"Look, when she shows up, have a heart-to-heart over a couple of pink girlie drinks with umbrellas."

He kissed her on the cheek and pranced away. There was no heart-to-heart. Al did not show up.

An uncomfortable film of sticky humidity coated her skin as daylight melted down the sky into orange pools that glowed on the roofs and trees of the Bermudan landscape. Absent-mindedly, she reached into her bag for a shawl to wrap around herself; a habit she had picked up from Al. Touching the spun silk ignited the autumnal vision of Al in a nimbus light tiptoeing into the art gallery. She glanced over to say something to her and was taken by surprise by the empty chair. Another one awaited her on the porch of the hotel after she made the long, slow walk home. Sitting on the steps waiting for Al but pretending not to be, she watched the moon until it landed in the middle of the tropical lace of palms holding out their fronds in the sky. They seem to have caught it there because when she arrived in the room and looked out the window, it was in the exact same spot. How could that be? It had to move. If it kept hanging there in the same spot, there would be no visual realization of night passing. A couple of proverbs came to mind about patience and the folly of giving impatient attention to anything: a watched pot never boils; there is not a tree in heaven higher than the tree of patience. Thinking had allowed her eyes to wander away from the sky and onto the ceiling. She snapped them back to the moon. It remained in the same place. She stared at if for so long that it put her in a trance until the morning sun caressed her eyelashes.

She placed her feet into a pile of crumpled papers from her attempts earlier in the evening write something to Al. On the nightstand she saw the half-empty bottle of wine next to a post-it. It had a confirmation number and the cost to send Al a bouquet of flowers.

Thank God her parents are in Europe. This would really be a mess if her parents were here, she told herself.

The crazy moon was shining brightly in the daytime sky and Jo wondered if it were a sign that things had not passed during the night as she had hoped they would. After showering and getting dressed, Al still clung to her thoughts. tried to predict the scene that would play out when she saw her. It was impossible. The scent of her hair and the sound of her voice were all around her and filled her with a joy that was almost palpable. She couldn't wait to see her. A knock on the door turned her eyes to the clock. It was 10:00 just when Al popped in mornings. Jo jumped up, but paused for a moment.

"Just a minute."

Then she flung open the door with cheerful "Hi."

There was no one there. Instead, there was a large bouquet of flowers in a vase. One of the housekeepers was walking away.

"Excuse me?"

The woman turned and Jo said, "I think there has been a mistake. I ordered these."

"Yes Mum. We delivered them."

"To room 737."

"Yes Mum but 737 checked out and told us to bring them here."

"Checked out? When?"

"Before the first shuttle bus, around 7:00 am."

Jo walked down the hall and handed the woman a tip for her trouble and went back to her room.

Mills would never let her live it down, and *that* was a scene she could imagine.

"Remember the time you bought yourself a hundred dollars worth of flowers?" he would and did ask.

"Really Mills would you let it go? You have done lots of things more foolish than that."

"Oh yes I have, and proud of it. I mean come on Jo. What are we going to talk about when we're older if we don't make fools of ourselves now?"

"Merry Christmas!" he said and threw a handful of confetti in the air.

"Merry Christmas. Where did you get it?"

"Queer bar. Come on."

He opened the bag and encouraged her to participate. They threw confetti in the air and met a few of his friends for a champagne brunch by the sea.

Before long, Bermuda had become a memory preserved in post cards and a few presentable photos that Mills had taken. She kept her thoughts of Al with them, tied in a raffia ribbon and tucked away in the privacy of a drawer.

Several weeks after returning, her little apartments seemed just that. The sunny rooms of Bermuda still blazoned in her mind's eye and made the Cambridge rooms seem darker than they usually did. In Faraway/Closeby the precise spot she thought she had found herself a couple of months ago, she was lost. One day the seas of her emotions rolled a crushing wave of loneliness and anxiety over her. She had to get out. She longed to be in the home she had made with Conrad among all things familiar. Impulse shot her out of the house and across the Cambridge Common to a cab. Within twenty minutes, she was there. At the back door, she pulled out her key and paused for a moment wondering if it would work.

Why wouldn't it?

In the garden, the Moorish fountain and withered ivy leaves flowed beneath the ice down to the frozen earth. Jo sat on the Italian marble bench in front of it, and recalled the day in Florence when they had purchased it. She and Conrad had gotten a fabulous deal, but they forgot to factor in the cost of shipping which was more than the bench itself. It was a story each had often told at dinners and cocktail parties. Everything was shades of grey in the cold winter air. Conrad's bike lay fallen in the brown grass by the house; the tires were flat. In between the spokes, the slim strands of light conspired with the mist to create a rainbow which brightened when the rain fell.

She and Conrad had talked more and more, together and with a marriage expert who was neither Dr. Allen nor his therapist. None of them would have thought showing up out of the blue was a good idea, and she contemplated leaving after she walked around the yard, but the rain encouraged her to go inside. She tossed her purse on the kitchen table and it slipped off. When she picked it up, she noticed it was new. The old table with its bad memory was gone. This one was beautiful. Curiosity pulled her into every corner of the house. It was still her house. Her books remained in the library. An unfinished canvas of a stunning figure eight that the sun occasionally makes in the sky, an Ana lemma waited on the easel to be finished. Even her old red silk Chinese robe hung on the hook on the bathroom door. All was neat and tidy.

Maybe he's gone away? she thought.

The fresh scent of laundered linens told her the bed had just been made, probably in anticipation of his return. She slipped on her flannel shirt and slid under the quilt to warm up. A large tag or piece of paper wafted out and fell on the floor. It was an old cracked photograph, a close-up of her that Conrad had taken a long time ago, though she could not remember where. Her bones ached as they did after a seventeen-hour flight that turned into twenty-four, but her bed comforted her; she allowed herself to fall asleep.

In the morning, she awakened in her bed and realized she had not really slept well in months. Though it was her house, it had become Conrad's space and she didn't want him to be uncomfortable. With some haste she dressed. Her phone rang and rang and rang, but she couldn't find her bag. She dashed downstairs, and the sound grew louder as she approached the kitchen. When she arrived, she saw Conrad holding her bag out. She dug the phone out and answered. It was Miller who was worried because he stayed at her apartment, and she hadn't shown up.

"I'm fine. Let me call you back."

Conrad asked, "How are you this morning?"

"I'm sorry I didn't mean to put you out. I thought you... I just needed to..."

The table had been set for two.

"Oh you're expecting someone. I should..."

"I got in late last night and you were zonked. I didn't want to disturb you...I was thinking about that sign of yours, Faraway/Closeby?"

"What about it?"

"I think I get it now?"

Jo sat down with him, Conrad, the charming, bumbling thoughtful geek she had married. He looked quite attractive in his unevenly buttoned Oxford shirt. He muttered about a lecture he was preparing to give, and then suspended his fork over his eggs and look right at her,

"Jo I have come to realize that certain aspects of the human experience such as physical pleasure and reactions of the heart, are simply beyond tabulation and quantification. . ."

"So when you told our marriage counselor you were socializing in an effort to gather data for enumeration or...something, you were serious?"

"Post facto, yes. Not deliberately mind you. I didn't intend to..."

"What did you conclude?"

"It isn't the collusion, but the spirit of the person with whom one is colluding. There are just are no patterns to give insight into such structures or activities, and this part of the human experience is impossible to analyze," he said.

She was not completely sure what he was talking about but she enjoyed how it made her listen and think.

I know what everyone else is going to say because we have the same conversations we have been having for thirty years, the same thing, the exact same words. I can never tell what Con will say.

The following week she sat waiting for Miller. At 12:30, he sent her a text advising her that he was changing their lunch place. On her way she contemplated her situation.

First Great Aunt Lilly's dubiously sage words came to her, "...courtship is the introduction, marriage the climax and divorce the conclusion. Right?"

Why? Is that a rule? 50% of marriages supposedly end in divorce, and of those who stay together 40% cheat. Why? she asked herself.

Among those she and Conrad knew who split up at eight months, five years or thirty-five years, the husband or wife, had declared the marriage over. It was "dead" or one had "changed," the couple had "grown apart," or one found the other "impossible to live with," "insane," or "a cheat," and on and on."

Once when the therapist had asked Jo what her reason would be for leaving her marriage she didn't have to think at all.

"My husband violated my trust...."

"So it wasn't the misstep?"

"Misstep? Boffing a co-ed in the kitchen is a 'misstep' to you?—Not technically, no. He is...was...the last person I would expect that from; otherwise I would not have married him."

Conrad shifted and pondered for a full minute.

"Leave? I don't want to leave. I never wanted to leave," he faced Jo and said, "That..." he waved his hands around, with the girl and the bike... it just happened."

"And all the party..."

For the first time since they had met, he shouted. "I didn't interrupt you Jo."

"Sorry."

"What was I supposed to do? You left! And all those women—not that I bedded *all* of them—but ...it was awful. None of them was you Jo." He faced the therapist, "so if—with a capital "I" left, the reason I would give is because I am only human."

"Jo!" Miller called, and then squinted his eyes at her and said with a sigh, "You are getting back together with Conrad, aren't you? You can't!"

"Nothing is decided?"

"I just hate to see you making a fool of yourself."

"Ha Ha. To quote you 'What are we going to talk about when we're older if we don't make fools of ourselves now?'"

"Touché Jo. Touché."

After lunch, Josephine felt again drawn to Brookline, to see Conrad.

"Did you notice the new kitchen table," he stammered out.

With a heart full of tenderness, she strode across the room and kissed him. Faraway/Closeby was far far away.

Miller eagerly took over the apartment on the Cambridge Commons, so he would have a place in town when he missed the train to Gloucester. Little by little, Josephine and Conrad slipped back into their life. Her upstairs studio was revived with linseed and paints, and she began a new canvas, her interpretation of the rainbows she had seen in the rain. Conrad resurrected his cycling hobby and even joined a club. Together, they went to art openings and academic functions. In private, once in a while, they excavated shards of events and emotions from the months leading up to their separation for clarification, understanding and prevention. Of the women he had dated, Jo asked if he had loved any of them. He was shaking his head before she finished the question. Of Allyriane, Conrad asked the same which surprised her.

"I felt very close to her," was all she could say.

One day in July, Jo went to tea with Miller at the former Faraway/Closeby. While the sign remained on the door, he had truly made it his. Sunlight was no longer allowed to barge in through the enormous windows, only to peek in between the lined paisley curtains when invited. The rays found his galaxy of crystal and the Neo-Baroque chandelier and refracted into stars on the newly papered walls. It was stuffed with heavy furniture from several periods which muffled the sounds. Miller set the kettle on the stove and then dashed out to the corner to buy cream for the tea. and pointed out the homo-erotic paintings he had recently acquired at auction.

"Look what I found at the store?" he announced merrily.

He tied back the curtain and let in the light, and then answered the call of the whistling kettle. Allyriane walked through the door. Neither she nor Jo spoke. Her unintentional push in Bermuda or Allyriane's abrupt departure and six months apart had created a barrier between them which would take more than a glance to tear down. Jo was struck anew by the soft natural loveliness of Al's face.

"Staying for tea Dearie?" Miller bellowed softly.

"Thank you, but no. I really can't."

Al retreated to the door which was still open.

"Another time," he said at the top of his voice.

"That sounds great," she replied. "I saw Mills. He told me you were here and we gave him a lift. I thought... to be honest, I don't know what I thought," she confessed and fidgeted with her fingers.

"You're looking well Al, a little..."

"Heavier. I know," she said and opened her coat to show her baby belly," five months."

"Congratulations! I am happy for you."

"Thank you."

"So you patched things up with Dom?"

A car horn blared and rushed her words, "We are together. I have to go."

Al pulled a card from her purse. Jo tried to take it, but Al held onto it while she finished talking, "I wanted to tell you...it was a beautiful Christmas."

"It was. Thank you

Al released the card to her and left. It read Allyriane and an email address embossed in gold. Jo went to the window. A black Cadillac idled by the curb in front of the building. A husky, grey-haired female chauffeur stepped out and opened the rear door for a woman who extended her hand to assist Al. She fell into her arms in a romantic lover's embrace, and they kissed. The woman slid into the car first. Allyriane raised her eyes up to the window and wiggled her fingers in farewell.

Miller bounded into the room drying his hands and standing beside her at the window announced, "Girls who kiss girls are lesbians or thespians pretending to be Lesbians."

"She just told me she went back to Dom."

"That's Dom, short for Dominique."

"No!" she gasped.

"Surprise. Miller gave her a little sideways hug, and they sat down to tea. Miller regaled her with amusing tales of auction acquisitions and men in bars. In the hallway, the sign clunked lightly on the door. Mid-sentence he got up and unhooked Faraway/Closeby from the door and handed it to her.

"Oh thank God you're here. I'm tired of trying to explain this."

The Picnic Table

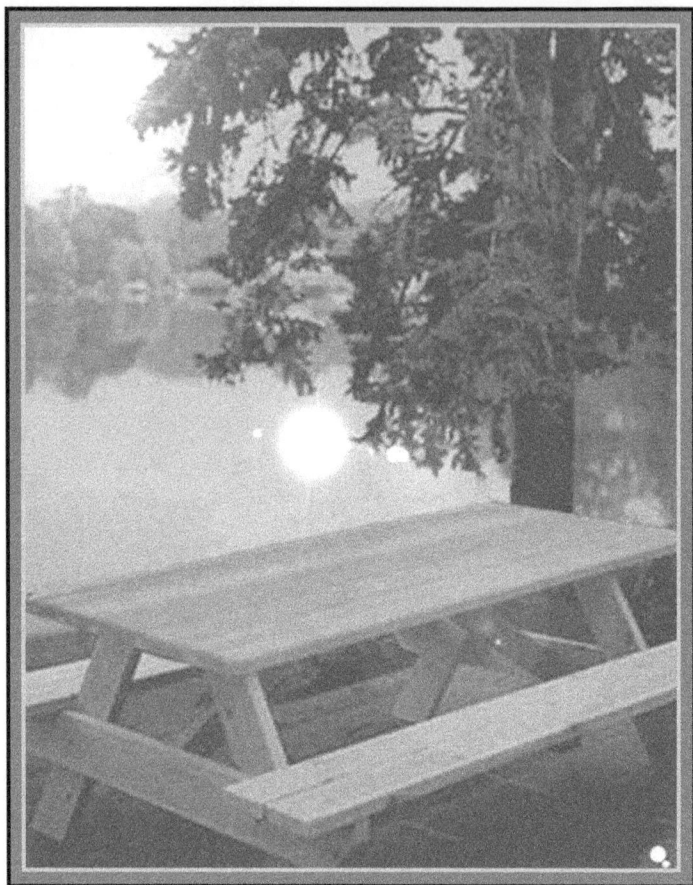

The Picnic Table

The picnic table was gone. Many things had been missing that week, including the top to the Osterizer, not the whole, black, rubber square, just the little, clear plastic thing-a-ma-jig that snaps into the middle and functions as a handle. It had been there for weeks of breakfast shakes and months of his newly-twenty-one sons' experimental concoctions. Tonight he needed it. He needed it immediately for mixed drinks. The boss loved frozen cocktails. He had arrived unexpectedly, not because he was not invited, he was, but the wrong day had been marked on the calendar. The boss always needed a drink with which to alternately pose and punctuate his monologue. He took a Kentucky Bourbon to tide him over until a mixed drink, his preference, was available. The booze splashed on the floor as he rocked back and forth in tasseled Italian shoes, while slyly eyeing the highlights of *Her* head. *Her*, his boss' companion, whatever *Her* actual name was, appeared from out of town, out of nowhere, the friend of a friend's friend, whose beautiful body New York's constellation of hotel rooms suspiciously could not accommodate with a single hotel bed. On the other hand, the sparse material of her dress understandably could not accommodate her breasts. A naked road of skin ran in an alluring path between them. Jealously cut his wife's eyes from it to her own Victorian-style blouse, and then to her husband's eyes, driving in reverse up the path to *Her* full carmine mouth. Turning right at its corner, his eyes collided with his wife's eyes. They glared a message to him before she left to answer the phone. She left "to change." She too needed a drink; they all did.

He had to find the little, clear, plastic, thing-a-ma-jig to assuage his wife's insecurity, to punctuate the boss' sentences, to give *Her* a glass full of less transparent liquid to hold in front of her and block that delightfully sensual but troublemaking path from his view and calm his own nerves. No one knew where the thing-a-ma-jig was. He called one of his sons. He directed him to call his brother who he was sure knew where it was because he had made a frappe with it two Saturdays ago when they were home. To his surprise, a girl answered his cell phone. Together they checked the number's accuracy before she explained she was "a friend of his son's roommate, but they went out and the phone was ringing and ringing, and it might be important," so she answered it.

"Where did he go?"

"Pizza. Wanna leave a message?"

"I'm looking for thing-a-ma-jig," he began, but the girl wanted to know how to spell thing-a-ma-jig .

After spelling and respelling, he hung up without any confidence that if she delivered the message at all that his son would understand and call back. He just knew somehow it was probably in his son's pocket, or his glove compartment, or his back seat beneath a stack of rarely, or never opened textbooks, or under a coed's taut young ass. He called his cell again, and she answered again. He told her he was going to call again and asked that she not answer the phone, so he could leave the message himself. He called. Out of habit, she answered. They laughed. He called. For fun, she answered. She laughed, he did not. On the third try she didn't answer, and he left the message. "Your brother said you're the last person who had the plastic thing-a-ma-jig for the Osterizer top, and I really need it. Can you get back to me as soon as you get this?"

"Any luck?" his boss' date asked with an open smile.

Remembering his wife's earlier glare, he knew he probably shouldn't take long to answer *Her*. He shook his head.

"If you were a thing-a-ma-jig, where would you hide in my kitchen?"

Her eyes twinkled more from champagne than flirtation and

she wound around expertly on her very high skinny heels. She lingered here, looked there and leaned into the dishwasher exposing a bikini line and a bit of the nipple of her left breast all at once. His wife would soon be changed and his zipper was getting hot. He reached out his large, soft, white-collar hand, cupped it firmly in place, pressed his palm against it, and pushed the red button marked crush. *Her* face lit up as she repositioned her dress to cover herself.

"Oh you found it."

"Terrific!" the boss said as he entered the kitchen and leaned against the wall with his arm over his head which made him stand taller, even look a little larger than he was.

"I suppose it was right where I said it was, wasn't it?" his wife muttered self righteously as she ducked under the bosses arm and into the room.

His eyes ran along the delicate lace pattern of the blouse she had changed into. It was a translucent pale blue dotted with rhinestones that sparkled all over. He remembered the last time she wore it, New Year's Eve in Martinique two years ago, how the shimmer made her stand out which she usually didn't. She possessed a button-nose, girlish prettiness and carried herself in the classical way of other sheltered girls who grow up to get their masters which they cutely called their MRS. if they haven't married by the time they graduated with their BA's. As with most, his wife's degree was in Art History, and Romance languages. She spoke just enough French, Spanish and Italian to talk to almost anyone anywhere; she was his own "Jackie Kennedy," he sometimes said. She was so smart she would never say anything more intelligent than her husband at a professional function or even with family and friends for that matter. She was undemanding and sweet, at least in public. She would provoke compliments, not comments. She looked as luscious in the revealing blouse in the kitchen as she did in the countless French negligees he had bought her to please him, to stimulate him into loving her again as he had a decade ago. They worked for his physical feelings but had no effect on the emotional. Nothing was powerful enough to escalate him above the years of petty bickering fueled by the pettiest of grievances, frustrations, routine, ennui, fears, envy and apathy which she had expressed openly. They hardly talked. At some point, she had changed from an innocently saucy co-ed whom he loved and loved to be with to a stranger.

Not even sex was a pleasure. He knew she wasn't interested in sex because she told him she wasn't, but she wanted to make the marriage work, "for the children." Her apathy and failure to initiate never deterred him from employing her body for self-gratification. She never protested, but as the years passed, her perfunctory and predictable praise for his performance annoyed him. Even when he pleasured himself, he could hear her blasé remark, "You were great honey," or "Thank you." He thought her virginal status at twenty was why she was so inanimate, embarrassed and puritanical in bed, but he hoped she would mature into a more participatory and enthusiastic lover. She never did. Before "they" became pregnant with their second son, he wanted to suggest sex therapy. Even if he had gotten around to talking to her about it, he wouldn't have had time. Working seventy hours a week and commuting had bought the house by the water with the picnic table; allowed her to stay at home and raise the boys; send the boys to private school and university and provide them with a vacation home and take them anywhere in the world on a whim. While material rewards and status were the trade-off for great sex with his wife, its absence weighed on his psyche and caused him to question his masculinity. With women in his bachelor days, he had had spontaneous, frisky fun in the back of the car, in an elevator, and a few times en plein air. Right after they bought the house, he persuaded his wife to try it on the picnic table, but getting her to agree took so much convincing that he almost lost the urge. Afterwards, he laid back to bathe in the moonlight, but she covered herself and scampered into the house and left him alone. He questioned whether he had married the right woman.

Her was a woman who validated his virility by the intensely seductive manner in which she did everything. Even the smallest touch sent blood rushing to his groin. *Her* aroused him from the minute their eyes met. He was combing his hair in the bathroom mirror downstairs when *Her* appeared. When she told him to sit on the toilet, he did. He felt light-headed when she gave him, "a little more relaxed hair style," and her fingernails ran along his scalp puffing up his hair. He wanted to slam the door shut and take *Her* against the wall. *Her* was not particularly beautiful, but she had the same something of countless other *Her*s whom he had met and screwed in fantasies and in the flesh on business trips and once on vacation along the way to today. He thanked *Her* for her efforts, restrained his desire, banged the door shut and hurried to the kitchen.

Her slipped in behind him as he stood with his hand on the Osterizer to make the frozen cocktails without the thing-a-ma-jig. He jumped nervously. His wife cut her eyes to *Her* so sharply that she backed away, and into the boss' arms.

Accusingly, his wife said, "You didn't answer me. "Wasn't it right where I said it was?"

He didn't recall her having said the thing-a-ma-jig was in any particular place. To show he had not found it, he raised his palm and in so doing released a shower of drinks that incited laughter from all, except his wife. He blushed at his blunder and suddenly felt contempt for the little, clear, plastic thing-a-ma-jig that fits in the middle of the top and functions as a handle. *There was a time when you would have laughed;* he wanted to say a loud.

***

The following evening when he arrived home, there it was. Just like that, the thing-a-ma-jig was right there. He picked it up from the faded, square where the picnic table once was and sighed in disbelief and confusion. Setting his briefcase down, he wondered where the picnic table could be. He wondered if his wife would believe him once again tonight about where he was earlier, as she had so many other nights.

Probably, he chuckled to himself, *but where the Hell is the picnic table? Imagine that. The whole friggin' picnic table was gone after twenty-three years.*

The ragged, bald square in the grass where the picnic table had been caused him to realize, he had come to take it for granted. The picnic table had once been so important. He and his wife spent one entire Saturday afternoon selecting it, a second moving it around the yard before they settled on the perfect spot and then a Sunday to reposition twice. With their arms around one another, the stood back and with great satisfaction viewed the final place it would occupy for two decades. With the addition of an enormous screened gazebo around, it drew the family out of the house and extended the area of their living room. Beginning in the spring and ending in late fall they enjoyed dinner al fresco. Guests were attracted to the outdoor setting as well. He saw the picnic table bending with the weight of dips, potato salad and ears of corn. Before the boys outgrew birthday parties, their cakes and gifts were centered there every June and August, so they and their rambunctious friends could run wild in the yard. The picnic table provided a place for romantic dinners and freed them from the familial fold. He could picture the table's stains and scratches, its weather worn surface. He knew it needed to be sanded. He said he would "get to it," a few times including recently in the car after his wife complained sweetly. "It's so rough honey, I have to cover it with a tablecloth and that gets ruined because...well as I said it's so rough," and showed him the spot from which she had removed a splinter. Not long after that, he again convinced her to make love on the table which, through the blanket they laid, snagged her hair. She tutted and stormed in the house. Then, yesterday morning while he ran his hand over it to check, he got a splinter in his own hand. *The table! I didn't fix it, so she sent it out,* he told himself.

This had certainly been a week for things to go missing. He noticed the bear, of the bull and the bear cufflink set, was gone on Tuesday morning at 6:15 am when he was getting dressed. He asked his wife if she could look for it. She said she had. He knew she hadn't. The white creamer shaped like a cow, which threw up milk into his coffee was gone on Wednesday. He asked if she knew where it was.

"Open you eyes and look for it," she suggested.

"My brother gave me that for Christmas, you know?"

"I do know. Maybe it ran away with the spoon," she said.

She laughed. He didn't. He brushed her comment off with the minutia of lint dust from his striped suit. To that end on Thursday, he had to use his tape because the brush had mysteriously vanished.

So Friday; the picnic table is gone. What next?

He shook his head bothered that it bothered him. Nothing usually did. at least that's what the guys at the office always said. Maybe because the picnic table was so large, it had this effect on him. The other things had come and gone and, and until the thing-a-ma-jig, he hadn't given them a second thought. This was different. One couldn't assume that a picnic table had gotten lost between the shirts, behind the cups, or in a shoe at the bottom of a closet. He pivoted in the bald spot on the grass and noticed that there was something particularly cold about the house, and he blamed it on the clouds covering the moon.

He opened the door. His keys jingled as he flicked on the light. Lackluster silence resounded from the dingy flowered wallpaper, accented by the steady drip of the faucet. His every movement echoed. His mouth went dry as his eyes fell on empty corner after empty corner of the counter, the floors, and the rooms. All the things that had once filled the house into a home were gone. By the sink, the lint brush was next to the cow pitcher. When he picked it up, the bear cufflink rattled along with its bull mate. He opened the cupboard out of habit to get a glass; an old plastic tumbler stood there alone. He filled it with water and walked outside to sit and think on the bench, but the picnic table was gone.

Five Wednesday's

Five Wednesdays

The woman at the end of the bar wore a strand of lustrous pearls that gleamed in contrast to her dark hair and black dress. The bartender hung back, assuming her companion would arrive presently as was usually the case with elegant women. When, after several minutes, she remained alone, he offered her a drink list. Nanette didn't like to drink by herself, but she had not intended to be alone, an occasion which called for "a nice cabernet." She sank into her private thoughts.

Well Sir Endipitous, you got me. Here I sit waiting for you like the fool that I am. Smart as I think I am, I should have figured any one who would make up a name like that couldn't be trusted. She glanced around the crowded hotel lounge and stifled the urge to address the patrons, many of whom were on their own. *Let's end the cloak and dagger cyber-socializing that is fictionalizing over our lives. Let's be radical and retro and be polite and personable, say hello in person, maybe chat and get to know each other the way we used to at our parents' parties and college mixers. Sir Endipitous...serendipitous. Strange. Serendipity is almost impossible to translate into other languages but not 'he stood me up.' Él me puso de pie. Il m'a fait faux bond. Mein Freund hat mich versetz. God. Why didn't I stay in Hamburg and tried to sort things out with Gareth?*

The bartender placed the goblet in front of her with a genuine smile and she felt more comfortable. "Put that on my tab," a scotch smooth, voice ordered over her head. The white check snapped in the air cutting off her objection as the bartender handed it to the rangy man. His square manicured fingers had no ring. Her eyes glided up his tailored, gray suit sleeve to his swarthy, dignified face. The slightest of jowls lined his jaw, and an aquiline nose stood prominently between two wondrously blue eyes enhanced by his shock of chestnut hair. She wanted to tell him, "I can pay for my own drink," but instead offered a nod of thanks and dismissal. He didn't leave. The buttons of his starched white shirt reminded her of Gareth whose dressing ritual included taking great care in lining them up. "When they are off, they are such a nuisance to unbutton and rebutton," he once explained smoothing his hand over the fromt.

✳✳✳

They had left New York for a long-postponed honeymoon through Europe, "to luxuriate in sin" and "compare new and favorite haunts," they told their friends. The truth was Nanette had become emotionally distanced from Gareth because his jealousy that she once found sweet had escalated into suffocating possessiveness. They were going to try to salvage their eighteen-month marriage by following their therapist's advice and spending "some serious quality time together to work things through." They were unified in planning, but their ideas were quite different. As a jumping off point, she had dreamily proposed, "Paris for the cafes, and we could tango on the Quai by the Seine, visit the Garden of Hopeless Romantics or stroll around Père Lachaise Cemetery to find our favorite dead authors and musicians." He proposed, "Pamplona, see the running of the bulls, stay where Hemingway did and..." her less than enthusiastic reply encouraged him to add, "and the cafes. The Spaniards have romantic cafes." They compromised and settled on Hamburg where each had spent many happy times.

In Hamburg, her skill in German, that was far superior to his, spun most of her interactions, even purchasing a scarf or confirming directions, into flirting. When they ran into the violinist, her former, younger, lover Werner whose sinewy, Teutonic good-looks Gareth had once overheard Nanette sum up to her girl-friends as "pure perfection...between the sheets too." It didn't matter that Werner arrived arm in arm with his head-turner, knockout of a wife, Angelica on whom he doted. The manifestation of Nanette's former paramour unleashed Gareth's suspicions, and to her great annoyance, crept into their post co-ital spooning with his questions as to whether he or Werner was the better lover and accusations that she still carried a torch for him.

Wednesday night she left Gareth behind "to catch up to the time change" and met the couple for drinks.

When she came back to the room, she mentioned casually that "we didn't do much, took a bit of a Reise in die Vergangenheit, you know, a trip down memory lane, and went on the Riesenrad."

"The ferris wheel," he chuckled.

"What's funny about that?"

"Awkward for you to be the third wheel on the ferris wheel, I guess."

"I wasn't. Angelica got a massive migraine and left, so it was just me and Werner."

All the skin on Gareth's body flushed bright red.

"It was just the two of you?! It's almost one in the morning. Did your little trip lead to a room?

"Don't be ridiculous."

When she turned to walk away, he did something he had never ever done, grabbed her by the arm. Shocked, she shook herself free from his grasp which left red finger marks.

"Gareth! What has gotten into you?"

"How would you feel if I went out alone with ..."

"I did not go 'out alone' with Werner. We ended up alone, and no matter who you went out with, I would not hurt you"

"As Mr. Shakespeare said, 'methinks the lady doth protest too loudly.'"

"The quote is, 'The lady doth protest too much, methinks.'"

"Don't change the subject."

Quite calmly, she left and arranged another room for herself. Fearful that Gareth might go and challenge Werner, she texted him. "Getting my own room. My arm is still red. Let's regroup in a couple of days. Try to sort this out," she reread the text, and tacked on, "BTW, I AM ALONE."

His reply was immediate but very brief, "K."

✳✳✳

During her respite, the painful truth erupted into the forefront of her ruminations. The catalyst for her second marriage to Gareth had not been love, or what, during those months, she thought was love, but certainty that another "good man" would not appear in her middle-aged widow's life and recalled thinking, "*At least Gar and I are friends.* On Wednesday, the third morning, in the nimbus of twilight before awakening, she slid her leg to the spot in the bed next to her; it was cold. She opened her eyes to the empty pillow where she usually saw him smiling sweetly in his sleep, and she genuinely missed him. With the incident nearly forgotten, she planned a kittenish move.

Stuffing her mischievous giggles down with the flurry of butterflies in her stomach, she tiptoed into their suite to tape a brunch invitation for Gareth on the bathroom mirror. His alluring scent hung in the air tempting her to join him, but she restrained her urges, sidled into the hall, and then stopped cold. The butterflies swarmed away. A petite young blonde wearing one of her lace robes, was about to flush the toilet. snatched the crotchless, bejeweled, panties the girl had left on the floor and tiptoed off unnoticed. *Those breasts! But a blonde. Pfft! He doesn't even like blondes. Or so he said.* She fumed to herself while she stuck a note with the lingerie, "I'm off. Talk at home in New York," automatically signed, "Love Nanette," and left them in an envelope for Gareth at the front desk. That night, while commiserating with Werner and Angelica, she received his reply, "K." They thought she should cancel the next leg of the honeymoon, but she insisted "Paris is just the therapy I need."

From Gareth's post cards awaiting her in New York, she knew he had also sojourned on to Spain, "See you soon. Love, Gar." *Love?* She scoffed. Had he followed the itinerary, he would have been in the seat next to her on the flight home instead of an airline blanket. Eventually, he arrived and texted to say he was "with Coburn," his brother, but he didn't come home which she attributed to his probably *having brought that bimbo back with him. That's why he doesn't answer the Goddamn phone.* Immersing herself in work for her arts foundation only partially cloaked the elephant in her life. Socializing within their circle of friends was out of the question. What would she tell them? Frustration and loneliness one particular Wednesday, escorted her to an online dating site that led her to the current Wednesday in the bar.

***

Several seats were free, but the man who bought her drink leaned on the back of her stool. She looked right at his face to see if he bore any resemblance to Sir Endipitous' which he did not. He threw her a big smile which she did not catch. "Excuse me," he apologized and brushed her shoulder, "there was a leaf and..." Nervousness tensed all of her upper body muscles. She focused on her breathing to calm herself enough to invent conversation. Not having eaten and he mounting anxiety she suppressed resulted in her swooning right onto the man, an act he interpreted as a positive reaction to his come on, but realized he might have misunderstood when, in the middle of his compliment, "I love your hair," she slumped toward the floor. Placing a tender arm around her, he guided her outside. He held her tightly while New York's people and traffic passed as if time-lapse blurs. Her purse, which he had gathered from the bar, dangled from his arm. It slid up and down as he stroked her back. "Just breathe. We're all a little tense, aren't we?" German marched to front of her brain and out of her mouth into the million-dollar view of the skyscrapers and penthouses.

"Was? Wer bist du?"

"Oh No. Do you speak English. "

"I do."

"Great. Are you all right?"

With a clear head, she assessed him to be a big American jock slash Wall Street trader. *He sure is handsome. Why not do something different just this once? Who would know?* But it wasn't his height or his eyes that made up her mind. It was his kind, nature and green advances.

"Do you have a car or shall we cab it?"

He jingled his car keys.

"Did you ever see a film about a man and a woman who meet and become lovers without knowing anything about each other, not even their names?"

Grinning from ear to ear he said, "Sure, Last Tango in Paris. That actress was stacked."

A flick of his wrist launched them into the galaxy of traffic. After a few blocks of silence, he began to talk, and he kept on talking and talking and talking about himself and how beautiful people were always attracted to him because, "birds of a feather flock together." Without any need for acknowledgement, he shared snippets of his earlier days as a ladies' man. Oblivious, she did not join in but watched the city lights kaleidoscope outside her window. He slapped the steering wheel. She felt his eyes on her. "God you are pretty. This is great." When they got out, a surge of pure sexual attraction pulled them together in a light kiss. "Damn it I can't park here. Come on Lord, I know I ask too often but seriously, tonight, I really need a space," and to her surprise, one opened up.

Suddenly she wanted to jump out, to run away from temptation, to be the woman who resisted, who wasn't interested, a permanent thorn in the side of the stranger's ego. They had not stated their intentions, and there were several cabs at the corner. It would be easy to hail one and never end their story before it started, but a sudden rain storm pushed her under the awning to his apartment building and sent the cabs off to collect fares. *This was a bad idea. I don't even know this guy.* The pleasantly inebriated, Wall Street Adonis with his dark ringlets and glittering eyes bounded up to her and folded her into his arms. She had never been intimate with a stranger, but when he shyly kissed the back of her hand in the corny gesture of a bygone era, he unwittingly, dispelled her misgivings. She dashed playfully up the stairs behind her. By the eighth floor, she was hoping he would call out that they had arrived. When he did not, she sat on the top step. He threw himself down and poked his head under her black dress. She squealed. His tousled head emerged from under her hem. "I love the rustle of soft fabric in my ears," he admitted and disappeared beneath it again evoking girlish resistance in foot stamping and shrieks. A woman in a housecoat peeked into the hall and called back inside,. "It's just that guy from across the hall."

In the apartment, they undressed themselves and each other without any further small talk or even a light. Their shoes thumped on the floor, a belt buckle clinked, sleeves whooshed, as their bodies commingled and lips were pressed to lips, cheeks to cheeks, breasts to chest and flesh to flesh in an erotic etude. The front door bumped too loudly, the rough stucco wall scratched painfully, so they resorted to the chair which was comfortable but weak. The leg snapped and without breaking stride they finally achieved sweet, sweaty release. Immediately they separated and retreated to a private space with a foot between them.

"God wasn't I great?" he asked breathlessly.

She rolled her eyes in the dark and listened to him slide along the carpet, clear his throat, fumble over knickknacks and click the room into the stark, unsexy glare of a 150-watt lamp bulb which he immediately dimmed. Assuming it was a rhetorical question, she remained silent and ran her fingers through the soft luxurious carpet. "Nice, isn't it? My wife, well ex-wife, and I got that an auction when we first got married. That was our thing, auctions." He paused as though he was daydreaming. She collected her bra from the top of a door, her panties from the coffee table and her dress from a chair, and went into the bathroom to put them on while he continued in the loud voice of a player on a football field, so she could hear. "I am so glad you're here. When my wife left, all of our friends took sides, mostly with her. You know. Of course, the guys were glad to be rid of me because their wives all loved me. I could have had any of one of them. It sucks that the guys didn't trust me cuz they knew I never would have cheated on my Linny. She was perfect."

She hurried out of the bathroom to encourage him to lower his voice and walked right into him.

"Would you help me find my shoes?

"Shoes? You're not leaving, are you? I thought we could get some food," he said and handed her a menu from a stack of take-out menus by the lamp.

She took it but checked the corners for her shoes.

"And I know you will find this hard to believe, but she left me for an older man, a much older man, and he was much shorter. Can you believe that? Look at me," he commanded and held his arms out to the side as he studied his physique in the full-length mirror. "I was All-American in college. I could have had any woman I wanted, but I chose her. Now that I think about it, I don't think I ever slept alone as an undergrad or graduate! I dare you to tell me I'm not the best you've ever had."

He was not, but she didn't say anything. She brushed her hair, and he poured himself a drink. "My wife said that old fart was an attentive lover. I'm attentive and virile," he proclaimed and slapped his chest. "I can get off three times a night," he bragged. "She said I should talk to a shrink as if there is something wrong with me. I'm not the one who lied. I'm not the one who snuck around. I'm not the one who cheated with a Goddamn senior citizen. Linny needs the shrink. God she had the sweetest ass. Anyway, we got the rug. . ." He returned to the story, but she didn't hear it; she tuned him out.

I have to get out of here.

"Hey Babe! Don't go," he said and embraced her very lovingly.

She saw her shoes, slipped them on, grabbed her purse and-dashed into the elevator, fortunately waiting. She held up her palm.

"You're naked."

Insisting she "Hold the elevator," he dashed into the apartment and back out with a shirt. "I like you. Let's start over. I'm Doug. What's your..."

The doors closed. The taxis' lights were on beyond the glass lobby doors and the rain had stopped. She wanted to walk and think. Doug carrying his shirt thundered down the stairs. "Hey!" She ran out and into a cab. Modesty held Doug behind the glass entrance while he slipped on his shirt before he stomped into the damp night.

"I'll be there on Wednesday. I'm always there on Wednesday."

Making contact with her in the rearview mirror, the driver shook his head and told her, "The driver's can't figure out what's wrong with that man. He lives up here, must have money, and he looks pretty good, but sooner or later, every Wednesday's he's out here. We call him 'Wednesday's child.'"

She laughed, "You mean like the nursery rhyme, Wednesday's child is full of woe."

"He sure is."

∗∗∗

A month later, Coburn called to ask Nanette if she would be willing "to meet Gar at my place."

113

"Why are you calling? Are there going to be lawyers involved?"

"No, nothing like that. He thought you might still be pissed, and he didn't want to get into anything on the phone. His therapist suggested a face-to-face meeting."

"Therapist?"

"Yeah. I was surprised too."

"I'd love to see him."

"Okay. I'm going out of town Wednesday, so you guys can have the place to yourselves."

By the time Nanette arrived, Gareth had decorated his brother's balcony with candles and arranged the chairs so it resembled a French café. There, they bumbled through the awkward reunion but then easily shared more openly than they ever had, even laughed over their separate honeymoon pictures. When he proposed couples' therapy, she agreed without hesitation. And they thought it best not muddy the waters by jumping back into bed right away, a decision almost foiled by their long goodnight kiss.

Vito

Vito

Vito resembled his Black Labrador, Rocky, the way some people said he did. Both had the same jaunty gait and athletic tone. But Vito also looked a good deal like his car, a Camaro. They were solid, attractive and well-molded, one intentionally by Chevrolet, the other accidentally by the luck of the Italian gene pool. He stretched his tan abdomen over the cool, wet, red metal hood moving a large, yellow sponge with both hands. Arriving at the windshield wipers, he stopped and held his posture for a moment, partly to reach up and adjust his aviator sunglasses and partly to reach out and touch the hearts of those he knew were admiring him.

They were there every Saturday behind the white, lace curtains of his own windows and those on the block. At his house, their hair was twisted and turned into odd shapes held with mousse and glop and lacquer. Their fingernails were drying to points in a rainbow of colors. Their bodies were packaged in innocently tempting tops and decently tight bottoms while their mouths engaged in mindless matters. They were invariably pulling strappy shoes from closets to match with their new, soft, silk frills. They placed them in soft mounds on chairs then coordinated them into outfits on the bed, on each other and finally on themselves in the mirror.

"Wait'll my Tony sees this," Sherry said.

"I'm too fat. This makes me look fat doesn't it? It does. You're taking too long to answer. I knew it did," Sharon commented while stripping off the sweater.

Vito had once been part of the Friday night dress rehearsal of Saturday night thanks to his baby sitters, his older sisters, a year apart, Sherry and Sharon and their girlfriend, the blonde bomb-shell, Dianne. Whenever people said her name, they broke into two distinct syllables pronounced Di-Anne. They would drag him into the chamber of changes, their girls' bedroom where they worked their cosmetic magic to become, what the society at the moment thought babes, to the rhythm of rock 'n' roll. In a hazy nimbus of perfumes and cigarette smoke, they molted and donned new clothes while popping brightly colored bubble. Tiny Vito would sit quietly in a corner bivouac pulling "Stretch Arm-strong's" arms watching pastel bras and fleecy, fluffy hair appear and disappear and appear again in their long, indecisive what-to-wear dance. Once, Di-Anne couldn't seem to make up her mind. Standing in an oversize pink sweater which hung to the middle of her paper-white pants covering her pencil thin legs, Vito looked at her and felt the excitement of the circus. He widened his eyes, pointed his child-chubby finger.

"Cotton candy," he squealed.

All heads turned to him.

"How cute!" Di-Anne declared and cradled his head in her up-per arms so she would not ruin her manicure. Her pink angora-covered breasts, which had already developed, smooshed around his face. He pressed his lips on her cleavage and blew hard.

"Hey, I think Vito's giving me a Bronsky," Di-Anne laughed, wiping away his slobber.

"Only five and he already knows what he likes," Sharon said.

"Well I'll need a guy that likes legs," Sherry announced while lifting her t-shirt to display her barely budding chest.

Dianne chimed in, "You're only twelve. You'll fill out. You're gorgeous. Good genes," she added. When Vito imitated Sherry, and as she often did, she planted a raspberry on his belly to make him giggle.

"I got no-body; and no-body got me," Sherry sang mirthfully.

The ritual dressing dance continued, but now and again, the girls didn't want him there. To get rid of him, they would toss his "Stretch Armstrong," into the hall, and he would run after it. His temporary eviction from the room with the white, lace curtains eventually became permanent. It happened in increments like along with the growth of his feet from a size seven to a twelve. First, the door was left ajar, and he was free to wander in and out as he pleased. Not long after he had grown out of his size nine shoes, Sharon came home in an irritable mood with a box in a thin brown paper bag which she threw on the couch for a minute.

"Always, Feminine, Protection," he read a loud and asked, "What's that?"

Which she dismissed with a flat, "Nothin."

Around that time, the door closed.

"Hey, we don't wantcha ta just knock and come in. Kay? Knock and wait a sec or call one of us to see if it's okay."

A decade later, with a few girlfriends and his first car, he rarely went near their room, so the knock-first policy posed no problem unless impulse pushed him in. That is what happened the evening his excitement over a brand new music cassette, swung open their door.

"Hey guys, look what I got."

"Close the door, Vito!"

He didn't. He stood in the frame with a confused look on his face. Everyone froze. Sharon was on the bed with a furry, white powder puff and a shoe ready to hurl. Sherry had a blow-dryer in her hand and modestly covered her. He quickly averted his eyes from his sisters and laid them on the golden goddess Di-Anne whose full breasts spilled over the top of a lacey, royal blue bra and matching panties at the top of her long, pale legs as she painted her toenails. The sight took his breath away and rushed blood to his face and body beneath his jeans zipper. His mind wandered back to when she would blow raspberries on his tummy as they locked eyes. Dianne's twinkled coquettishly, and his lip turned up in a shy smile while he crossed his legs and quickly pulled his sweatshirt down in the front.

"Hi ya Di-Anne," he said softly so his voice wouldn't crack.

"You're supposed to knock!" and "Close the door!" his sisters shrieked.

Di-Anne ran her gaze down his body to his bulging sweat pants, and he pulled the door closed. The shoe and the can of powder hit the wood from the other side. The girls' voices lowered to titters and whispers and though he was only in the hall, he felt as if he had been dropped into a deep hole in the earth.

"Like all of the sudden, Vito is all grown up," Di-Anne noted.

"He can get as tall as he wants; he is still our little brother, right Sharon?"

***

The girls continued in life which took them separate ways. Di-Anne's desirable physical assets placed whatever she wanted within easy reach. At the restaurant she had the pick of hours which provided her with overly generous tips and male companionship from boys and men who offered her gifts unobtainable, sensual and material "the moon," "sexual ecstasy," to "a trip around the world." The more she refused, the harder they tried, but she rarely saw anyone more than once or twice, except young Vito who she saw almost every day when he stopped by for a soda, "on the house." He enjoyed being the object of the men's jealous faces when she fawned over him and kissed his cheek. Invariably, there was always one who asked if she was "robbing the cradle?" Holding Vito tightly, she joked, "If I could, I would." Eventually she met a balding, film producer, twice her age who, to her amusement, bought her anything she admired, in passing, including a white, convertible Mercedes and an enormous diamond belt buckle whose genuine jewels spelled out Di-Anne. She was the only woman Vito had ever seen blowing bubble gum and wearing a fur coat which she wore the last time he saw her before she headed out, "to the Coast," He got a mouthful of mink when she hugged him tightly, and he inhaled her aroma. Tears welled in her eyes.

"Di-Anne, what's wrong?"

"Nothing Vito, just..." she bent down and very close to his ear admitted, "In my heart, I don't want to go."

"Why? Don't you love that old guy?" he asked in an equally low tone.

"But... I could."

Doubt scrunched up his face, and he took her hand. "You should always listen to your heart."

"Well aren't you wise beyond your years?"

"Not really, my grandmother told me that..." He shuffled back and forth. "If you stay, we could ride our bikes over to the park. Go so fast the wind will blow are hair back like flags."

"That sounds nice. Next time. Okay?"

***

The passing years, relegated Di-Anne to an occasional memory when she wrote or called his sisters. Sherry and Sharon envied the luxurious California lifestyle she reported; even though she complained it was "actually kinda boring," and "not all it's cracked up to be."

"I spend my life getting dressed for lunch. I never know what anyone is talking about, and even if I do, no one wants my opinion."

"I would be happy to sit there and be quiet," Sharon covered the phone and told Sherry. She rolled her eyes and advised Di-Anne to "Quit complaining. It's better than working forty hours a week. We'd probably do anything for a life like that."

"Including watching a flabby, bald guy with grey hair all over his chest get naked and crawl in bed with you?"

"Send me a ticket and I'll let you know," Sherry chimed in on the extension,

Sharon had become an executive administrative assistant which she blamed for having plumped up so much. Her life was work, drinks, occasional dating and movie-going. *An Officer and a Gentleman* was her all-time favorite; she and saw it eight times and after every one, her face was always tissue-rubbed red.

"I wish a handsome naval officer would come into my job and carry me off to a wonderful romantic life the way Zack did Paula."

"Not exactly a movie that speaks for women's liberation."

"I like it for the romance. Sherry. Don't you believe in romance?"

"Sure I do, but if you're going to dream, dream for reality not fiction. Richard Gere could come and carry me off…just for an afternoon. Hell I'd settle for an hour," Sherry admitted.

Before seeing *An Officer and a Gentleman* a ninth time, her dream was realized when a trainer in the Officer Candidate School, Jimmy Grasso fell head over heels for her. Because he was divorced and older, she was not equally smitten, but she liked him "well-enough." Jimmy sensed a break up after being strung along for a year, so he decided to play what he hoped was the ace up his sleeve and secretly arranged for life to imitate art. In his dress Navy uniform, he walked into her office one afternoon, swept her up in his arms and carried her out. When she cried in disappointment because everyone was out to lunch, he repeated the performance and even trumped the scene when he sat her on the desk, dropped on bended knee and proposed. She accepted. They married, bought the house next to their mother's, but when he was away, she often returned to her childhood bedroom

Sherry had been the first to tie the knot a few months after high school graduation, with Tommy Prince, who had joined the army. She flaunted her PX card as if it were a gold charge card. He was supposed to ship out to Stuttgart, Germany, so she tortured herself once a week with German lessons which were all for naught because when the transfer came, it was to Korea.

Young Sherry didn't have the necessary maturity, commitment or love for her teenage husband to endure isolating military life, kimchee and cold winters for two years. By opting to stay behind and wait, she unwittingly became an understudy to a sweet Korean girl. Eighteen months later, Tommy filed for divorced and filled Sherry with self-loathing for not having been a more supportive wife and given the marriage a real try. Drinking at the bar subdued her guilt and brought her a second husband, Mike, a construction worker.

"Get over that guy already for Christ's sake. And quit telling people you have Triskaidekaphobia. They're gonna think you got a weird disease," Sharon advised her. "And come home! Di-Anne will be here any minute."

Di-Anne remained single. The old producer two-timed her with someone younger who he married. She decided to make a scene at his office, but he wasn't there; his new assistant was.

"He's out with his wife. Is there a message?"

"Actually it's something for her. I'll leave it on his desk."

The phone rang cutting off any objection from the assistant. Di-Anne wanted to write on the wall with lipstick but knew it would be too easy to dismiss as an angry paramour's revenge. He had a change of clothes in the office, so after carefully applying a heavy coat of lipstick, she planted kisses on the front of the shirt, and the zippers of the pants and the lapels of his light-colored blazers.

"You bitch! Your stupid stunt almost cost me my marriage, which would have cost me plenty for fuck's sake," he screamed at her when he blew through the door. And so, after all those years, she learned he had a wife. To her amazement, he tried to salvage the relationship with Di-Anne. "Try to understand. She was pregnant. I had to marry her. Now look, in order for this to work..."

"You would have get a divorce and not cheat on me."

Fear of gossip encouraged him to offer her thirty-five thousand dollars and a first class ticket, "Back to wherever the Hell I found you." She felt she could have gotten more but then it would be black mail rather than a gift; she did have him throw in a week in Hawaii.

Twenty-seven, dumped and feeling stupid, she returned to her former life. Sherry and Sharon's mother, Mrs. Salesa waddled out of the kitchen in a flowered dress covered with an apron. A wooden spoon in her hand dripped with sauce.

In her thick Italian accent, she said, "Dianna, you look like a movie star. Go! Go! Go to the room. Sharon is coming. All my girls will be here. Like old times."

The house seemed dark and small compared to the large, sunny houses of California but it had a comforting feel that allowed her to breathe easily. In the room, she flipped through a huge pile of photographs on the dresser. Several featured an eye-catching hunk, and she was eager for the girls to tell her all about him.

Sherry came in followed by Sharon two minutes later. As was their habit, they kicked off their shoes and sprawled on the bed and talked.

The girls went through the photos one by one and gave a detailed account of who was there and what had been going on in their lives. Finally, they got to one of Sherry with the young hunk. Di-Anne, tapped her nail on the photo.

"Don't you look cozy. What is he?"

The sisters exchanged a glance and burst out laughing with such gusto that one of them snorted a bit.

"God Di-Anne. How long have you been gone? That's Vito!"

"Vito? No way. I thought he had blonde hair."

"Some people grow out of it," Sharon told her.

Di-Anne blushed, "Oh my God, little Vito?"

"Little? He's gonna be twenty-one!"

"Don't tell him what I said. Okay?"

"We're not promising anything," Sherry teased.

Mrs. Salesa called the girls and they ran to see what she wanted. Di-Anne heard his voice, and she looked through the Venetian blinds. There was the hunk, Vito. As always, he was doing something to the Camaro he had just gotten from his family as a high school graduation gift. He liked to be seen near it, so he called out to anyone he knew and a few people he didn't as they passed.. He saw her and waved. As he carefully detailed the Camaro with a little brush he had purchased just for that purpose, he filled up with a warm feeling that almost sent him running to the house. He stifled it, so he could be cool. During her three-year absence, he had several fantasies about her, one of was quite simple. He wanted to take Di-Anne for a ride in his car like every other guy. Any would be willing to drive her clean across the Atlantic Ocean to Paris if she asked. He didn't want to take her anywhere in particular, he just wanted to blast down the highway and glance over and see her blonde hair whipping across her smile. He hopped over the side of the door and slid behind the wheel, and then wiped off the fingerprints he made. The radio volume went all the way up to twenty-five, and that was where it was when he hit the "on" button. All the birds flew out of the trees. Several neighbors stepped outside too. "Sorry," he called out and turned it down. He noticed a smudge on the windshield and got out to wipe it off. It was perfect. His mother's friend was driving up across the street.

"Vito! Vito, hi!"

He looked over his aviator sunglasses and posed proudly in front of his gleaming Chevrolet chariot. She said something, but he couldn't hear. So he took a step toward her. Just then, an aqua blue pick-up truck jumped over the hill and burst onto their street. For a split second, a blur of blue screamed toward Vito and the Camaro. The truck's rubber wheels caterwauled to a burning, stinking halt. Vito's jaw fell open. His tongue came out. If he cried out, it was silently. He was in a crumpled heap half-visible beneath the truck's chrome bumper. The loud music was warped as if it was coming from a passing vehicle. A sun-weathered construction worker leaped out of his truck and called excitedly at the top of his voice.

"Oh my god. He came out of nowhere. Kid! Hey Kid! Are you

all right Oh my God!"

Vito could hear phrases spoken by voices in the crowd asking, "What happened?" and "Is he dead? For an instant, he wished he was. How embarrassing. He wanted to spring to his feet and say something clever, but he had been knocked out and his brain was on hold. The gravel dug into his back; the comments continued. "Did you call 911? If you did, then I won't." "He looks dead." "If he isn't dead, don't move him." "Don't give him any water." He opened his eyes, and he saw a blur of faces. He recognized old Mr. Luna from up the street and a generation away.

"Nope, he's not a military man. You can always tell a military man."

He heard the rapid banging of high heels and a clattering of bangles which he knew belonged to the girls. Di-Anne sat on the ground and placed his head on her lap. Sherry handed her a bag of ice. Sharon gave her the glass of water, and in a big loud voice, she bossed the crowd.

"Back up. Wouldya back up? Give my brother some room, please."

"Here, have a sip," Di-Anne said softly and kissed his cheek tenderly, the way she did at the restaurant. He opened his eyes and nuzzled into her steamy lap. After he took a sip of water, a round of applause went through the onlookers. He took another sip and they clapped again. The driver helped him to his feet. Once he was up, the crowd shuffled lethargically off without further comment as if disappointed. Di-Anne kissed his cheek again. Other than an abrasion on his forehead and a bloody elbow, he was okay.

"You should go to the hospital and get checked out," the driver told him.

"Naw, I'm okay."

They exchanged information.

"What were you doing in the street anyway?" the driver asked running his eyes over Di-Anne's breasts.

"Are you finished," she asked, and he turned to Vito.

"Detailing my car, you know?" he said and swooned.

Rushing across the street, Sherry yelled, "Ma! Ma! Vito got hit by a car!"

His sisters' announcement clouded his face with dread for the drama they were building by calling out to his mother. The driver gave him a pat on the back and walked over to someone he recognized. Vito didn't see his mother yet, but he heard her.

"Vitale? Mio Dio. Vitale! Cosa è successo? Cosa è successo!"

"Oh man. I can't handle this. Why did they do that?"

Di-Anne went in Vito's pockets which made him squirm, and he shot her a wry smile.

"What are you doing?" he asked and laughed nervously.

She pulled out his car keys and held them up. "If you really don't want to deal with it..."

"You're kidding?"

He scrambled to his feet and hopped in the passenger side of the car. The radio blasted as they took off. In his rearview mirror, he his mother waving her arms and shouting in Italian next to his sisters with the first aid kit and a blanket He glanced at Di-Anne whose golden hair whipped across her face. She touched his thigh.

"Are you sure you're okay?"

Vito smiled at her and said softly, "Yeah. I'm sure," and he planted a quick, nervous kiss on the back of her hand, "Welcome home Di-Anne."

Winter Revelations

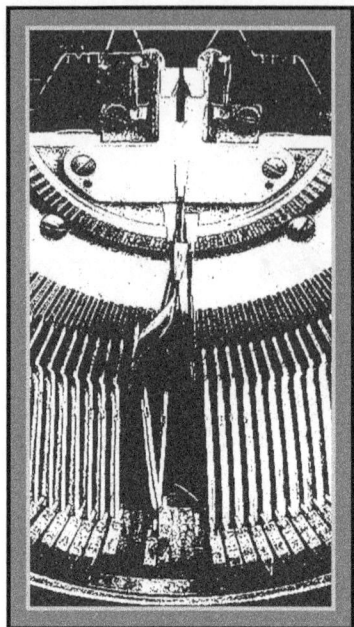

Winter Revelations

New York, 1978

Manhattan's Goliath grey buildings blocked out all but a little square of cold, winter sky dwarfing everything in the streets and rendering me an insignificant dot of humanity on the hard cityscape. There, the nameless, faceless masses hurried past as rapidly as the endless electricity that gushed through the hordes of wires. It colored the air blue, emitted a distinctly fluid *bzzz* that I heard above the ubiquitous cacophony of sirens wailing, subway cars rumbling, men working in the streets, dogs barking, and people talking. The bzzz was even louder when I was not occupied with friends or shopping or Val, my husband was away on one of his long work trips to a faraway place.

Mornings when he was not dreaming in our bed; evenings when he was not unwinding with a drink; weekends when he was not crooning in his Frank Sinatra style, making me laugh, as only he could, and nights, when he was not holding my hand beneath Central Park's century old wisteria vines, that bzzz haunted me. In his absence, I kept busy and kept my walks to Broadway on the upper west side where the fluid blue bzzz merged with all the other cacophonously tangled city sounds. Once, I stood attempting to single our one sentence and make sense of it. Gio, our beamy, old doorman flashed a face full of amused understanding and blared at me, "Ha! Give it up Doll. You'd have more luck trying to a listen to a sermon in a bowl of alphabet soup. Come on in where it's quiet." As he had for count-ess others over the past thirty something years, he swung the big, glass, door open for me.

I thought his enormous pleasure in opening and closing the door was a façade, but one night after he had had a few belts and was lying around off duty in his lounge, he confided in me. "I love this job. I really do. I can smoke my cigar. I am free to come and go, walk around, do stuff like walking and helping people." He considered himself more of an assistant or therapist than a doorman because in addition to his expected duties of hailing taxis, caring for dogs, ringing for the elevator, carrying luggage, running to the store or providing umbrellas, he was a sounding board for angry or despondent spouses; a confidante for stood-up dates; a companion for insomniacs and a supportive arm for those who returned pie-eyed. Over time, he had furnished the area behind the high sign-in counter with a "perfectly good" couch and an armchair that someone had left behind and brought in a record player, a radio, a TV, and a hot plate, and of course, there was a small well-stocked stocked bar. All tenants were welcome at any time. My neighbors agreed the familiar sight of Gio with his lounge, hidden in plain sight, gave a homey feel to the otherwise cold marble lobby. He was, indeed, as wel-come a sight as a beloved uncle when I returned from weeks of research in Sweden that had extended into Jul, Christmas. That threw off my biological clock.

I would be finishing my "Opera Libretti as Drama" midterm in a cranky, sleep-deprived haze. Researching and analyzing the topic shipped me to a place where I rarely go, the left hemi-sphere of my brain. In order not to be penalized a full grade, the paper was due in advance of Monday's 5:30 p.m. That knowledge and fatigue prevented me from accepting Gio's invitation to "Grab a seat and tell me all about it," and just presemt him the Dala horse he had requested for his granddaughter and a bottle of Akavit for his bar before going upstairs. I wished Val had been there to greet me, but the memory of a candlelit Scandinavian night we had shared a few weeks earlier when he popped up to Stockholm led me into a contented sleep and kept the fluid blue bzzz at bay. Typing would keep it there.

The typewriter was great for that. The clack clickety-clack clack- clack clickety-clack clack told me I was moving forward in my task. A bit of force was needed to return the carriage, strike the letters, the space bar and the shift key, so it engaged me physically. Though I first wrote all my notes for papers and stories in long-had, they always changed in the process of typing unless I was pressed for time. I wanted to be done with the paper and meet my friends to share our vacation debriefing which was invariably interesting and spirited. We always met at Tom's Diner on 112th.

***

On any given day and at almost any given hour, the diner sizzled with deep philosophical exchanges, political summits, romantic declarations and on and on through the canon of friendly intellectual, and often entertainingly shallow communication. My artsy, university, klatch, mostly foreign, whom Val called "the Europeans," had amusingly, powerful nationalistic feelings about what they ate and drank. To them, American bread was too airy, vegetables tasteless, beer watery, meat stale and full of poisonous preservatives and the coffee too weak. "American coffee is not coffee. It is hot, brown water," was the most-oft repeated complaint, even if we dined at the finest American spots. Though Czech, British and Portugeuse, all insisted their coffee or method of preparation was superior, and they did this in their home countries as well. Friends in Sweden claimed Swedish coffee "the best in the world." To blend Swedish coffee into the brew of criticism among my coffee connoisseur friends, I bought several bags as Christmas gifts. They were wrapped and ready by my door. As soon as I finished the requisite 25-page-minimum paper with footnotes and a bibliography, --Argh-- I would meet them.

I adjusted my chair, checked the ribbon, wound in a piece of paper and tapped all the way through to page nine before a wave of jet lag dropped my head back on my cushion. Intending to catch a few winks, I stretched out on the couch, but I awakened hours later. To restart my routine, I needed coffee, but the only coffee in the house was that which was wrapped. I had to go out. In the lobby, Gio was busy in his lounge, but as soon as he heard me, he dashed to open the door.

"Get out your galoshes Doll. Storm's coming."

"Thanks Gio."

The cold air slapped me in the face and I questioned his prediction. *Storm? It is much too cold to snow. And it is much too cold to go far.* Halfway to the corner, the fluid blue bzzz chimed in and rushed me there and back. It continued zzzing in my head. If I talked to Val, it would stop, it was the wee hours of tomorrow in Paris, but I rang him anyway to chat, perhaps a little pillow talk for him. I asked for his room, « sept, trios, cinq, » but to my surprise instead of his sleepy satin voice, a breathy and divinely feminine voice answered.

« Allo oui? »

I assumed the operator had connected me to the wrong room.

« Bonsoir. Est-ce cette salle 735? » I asked.

« Oui. »

Not the answer I wanted.

« Est Monsieur Lambert ... »

« Val? Oui, mais il est à la recherche d'un tire-bouchon »

« Un tire-bouchon? »

«Oui. Y a-til un message? » she snapped impatiently.

I did have a message, but at that moment, I could not muster the necessary French to say, "What in God's name is that woman doing in your room after midnight?" His position as an international, geological engineer afforded him lots of opportunity to attend conferences, and I had always trusted him. *When are you going to stop being so gullible?* I asked myself. Without more information, the events in that hotel room thousands of miles across the Atlantic were an unknown that held the potential for hours of dangerously destructive speculation. I envisioned her as a homely coworker and then a skinny, sexy, French girl in a flimsy, white blouse unbuttoned to her waist. *Hmpf.* I compartmentalized my fears and turned my thoughts to the paper, but that infernal fluid blue bzzz found me. Bzzzzzz

Just as I wound page ten into the typewriter, the phone rang. It was Val. We exchanged the usual pleasantries about the weather. He asked about my flight home and confessed "the conference is really great, of course. It's in Paris." Then there was an uncomfortable pause. I was thinking about the French-speaking woman who answered his phone, and I sensed he was too, but neither of us mentioned her. "I miss you," we said simultaneously and then blathered on for a few minutes before saying, "See you soon." For some reason the sound of a kiss he planted on the mouthpiece resurrected my trust in him however, it was shaken again because before I was able to rest the receiver in the cradle, I heard the French woman singing out, « Et-tu prêt? » and his voice shushing her. *Why? Why had he shushed her? If she was just a friend or a friend of a friend, why should he care if I heard her voice? Does that mean she was more than a friend?* I reminded myself that not doing well on the paper could jeopardize my grade and stemmed any residual negativity I had over the anonymous French woman, but apparently, it also churned in my soul which became evident when my typing turned too vigorous and angry-handed for the letter bars to keep up. They merged into an irreparable bouquet of metal letters over the roller. Damn it!

I was wide awake and angry and someone was pounding on my door. No one slips by Gio, so he must have recognized a friend and cleared him to come up. The familiar sound of heavy footfalls in front of the door accompanied by the accented muffled speech and giddy laughter announced, "the Europeans" before I even asked.

✳✳✳

All but Karel attended the School of International Affairs, though he was better versed in world history and politics, than the rest combined. His halting English improved to the brink of fluency when he drank, which was often, but none of us knew where or what he studied or even if he was a student at Columbia, not that it really mattered. He dressed in velvet jackets and when liquor elevated him above his naturally reticent nature, he was a brilliant conversationalist. Nigel was British, and in his blazer, easily, the most conservative; Mateo "Portuguese-Brazilian" and a self-described playboy who dressed the part in flashy brightly-flowered polyester shirts that clung to his well-toned torso and custom made gabardine trousers, most refined American men would have found too tight. Ariel was as gay as a flock of flaming pink flamingoes, and he thought he hid his proclivity despite his fondness for leotards accessorized with jangling clip earrings and a little mink jacket his mother had cast out. The festivity-seeking Europeans promised to be a long distraction, but the typewriter was broken and it was too cold to turn them out. After a mishmash of hellos, Karel, lost his hold on the doorframe and fell; the others dominoed into the foyer on top of each other. Their faces were rosy with liquor, probably ludes and mirth. Ariel lifted his pretty face from my shoe.

"Oh do you have a pair like this with a higher heel?"

"No, but you're welcome to have a look. "

I led him to the closet to choose among the few pairs I was willing to let him borrow which really meant *have.* Any pair I lent him walked away never to return. His request for heels and the others' fashionable garb told me they were headed for a club, have a last hurrah before classes resumed. Karel grumbled from the kitchen. Ariel and I clomped in to see the rest of the crew exchanging mischievous glances and stifling chuckles while they observed Karel. He was shaking his cherubic ringlets, searching his jacket pockets and slurring something. "We're not going to Xenon, agreed?"

We all had our favorite clubs; although I would tag along to any place that had massive speakers. They roared the music out at over 100 decibels and successfully vanquished the fluid blue bzzz. All clubs were relegated to second best when Studio 54 came into being, but its intense popularity and hyper-discriminating bouncer reduced non-celebrities and the less-than-fabulously dressed from ever seeing the inside, so we had to have a second pick. Ariel wanted to know "What is wrong with Xenon?" Karel declared "It's a dump? We're not going there, agreed?" Xenon was hardly a dump. It was a great disco on 43rd Street that pulsed with as many attractive, scantily-clad Go-Go boys as with Studio 54, but it just wasn't "the place." From his pockets, he produced his keys, wallet, rolling tobacco papers, Binaca breath freshener drops and a diminutive bottle of Absinthe which he held on high. He straightened up, clicked his heels and saluted it.

"He loves kissing the Green Fairy," Ariel said in a hushed tone, "and he has bonafide absinthe, the one with the hallucinogens, not the 'cheap knock-off swill you get here."

"Where did he get it?"

"Prague. He hid it in a leather wine bladder. Customs didn't catch it."

From the interior of his coat, Karel brought to light: a half-burned candle, a pair of socks, a pet rock and a small x-ray which raised eye-brows all around. Then he turned both pants pockets out and sent a shower of condoms flying and released peels of merry laughter from the guys Among the Trojans was a crumpled photo which he picked up with the utmost care.

"My Anezka!" he said and exhaled completely.

"Not yet, and she was mine first," Mateo teased.

"You never slept with her."

"I could have."

"Or so she made you think."

Thankfully Mateo abandoned the topic because competitions over women created intense disharmony. The pretty girl in the photo had cherry-red, hennaed hair that hung in springs of curls beside her pale, high cheekbones and round blue eyes; she was striking. "After tonight, she will be mine," Karel muttered. The Europeans eyebrows raised, and they exchanged discreet glances of curiosity, for they had assumed he was in the closet. Despite his sexy accent, disarming smile, and shy charm, no one had ever known him to have a female companion. Ariel had made an overture to him one night by suggesting they could "make beautiful music together." Karel's reply was that he did "love music," and that "My favorite instrument is the triangle." Because that was vague and confusing the Europeans hatched the scheme to further test his sexuality and set him up with Anezka, one of Mateo's numerous female friends. "We told her all about you, and she is dying to meet you," Mateo told him. Karel's face lit up when he heard her name. "Anezka? Is she Czech?" All Mateo knew was that she had a cute accent. With sad consistency, the petite beauty failed to appear at the diner, the steps of Butler Library a club, wherever they reported she would be. I sensed the set up might be sophomoric foul play, but I kept out of it.

I waited until after Ariel had selected a pair of shoes to rush the boys out, explaining I had to do the paper and the typewriter was on the fritz. Nigel took my arm. Morality caused me to take a step back because our long-time friendship veiled a simmering attraction that, with our significant others away, might lead to an affair. He lowered his head toward my ear and spoke softly, as though he was sharing the most sacred secrets of the universe. He claimed that the Europeans, "without at least one hot bird will never get passed the doorman. Ariel doesn't count." I burst out laughing.

"Ha! Sweet flaming Ariel is your ticket."

"Aren't you still on Swedish time and wide awake? Come with us.

"Where is Eliza?"

"She's still in England?"

"Well, a fiancées doesn't want her beau out with…"

"Fiancée?! Wrong love. Eliza is not my fiancée."

"No? Haven't you been together for…? Anyway Nigel, I have repair the typewriter."

"None of the shops can do it on short notice. Why don't I bring one by…"

"Tonight?"

"I was thinking, late tomorrow."

"I don't know. Procrastinating makes me anxious."

"Tardiness too. You read me the riot act for being late…"

"Only the umpteenth time."

"I had an excuse."

"Right your apartment key was glued to the table."

"Who leaves his apartment unlocked in New York City?"

"Who glues his key to a table?"

"As I said, It was an accident. I was repairing the leg, and…"

"All right. It doesn't matter now Nigel. That was years ago.?"

He glanced over the typewriter at the thoroughly jumbled keys.

"I can always write it in long hand. Professor Lipman will accept it."

"That's silly. Whether you come with us tonight or not, I will bring the typewriter, but I think I can persuade you to come."

He flashed a fan of shiny, gold VIP tickets for Studio 54. Having them meant not standing outside and freezing while the smug, overly-critical doorman decided if we were up to 54's requirements. The tickets bolstered my feeling that I would be a crummy friend not to go along. Besides, miles away, the black dawn of Swedish winter was breaking, so my body was telling me it was time to begin a new day.

However, staying on European time, I would be further exhausted, not at my best to work. At the last minute, I tried to back out by complaining that "I don't want to rumple my dress."

"Don't be such a bore," Ariel chirped. "Mateo's father sent a limo, right?"

Mateo nodded and handed Karel a few condoms he had missed when collecting those that had fallen from his pocket.

"In case Anezka is there," he said with a smirk.

Karel shrugged off his attempt to rile him with "If she is, she is," and again saluted his Absinthe bottle before swigging.

With a warm, chic comfortable ride, guaranteed entrance with the VIP tickets and of course, Ariel. I had no way out of having a good time. Ariel was outfitted in sequined white spandex pants, my clear plastic Cinderella platform heels from last Halloween, the lush fur and enormous, pink, rhinestone-studded, dark glasses. He stepped out first and flamboyantly hammed it up for a few with cameras who mistook his unrestrained ostentation for celebrity and caused the doorman to rush out to welcome us. As he escorted us through the crowd straining to see who had arrived, we heard guesses of "Bowie," and "Jagger." Entering the club was like stepping onto a super-sized, cruise-ship. The atmosphere sparked vivaciously in the night as it sailed the coast of Fête Fantastique. The space was enormous, maybe two or three hundred feet in both directions and a ceiling beyond the balconied floors with partiers on each one. Committed exhibitionists, including Ariel sparkled in every corner.

Mateo had frequented 54 since the grand opening, and his reputation as a handsome, generous ladies man and fantastic dancer was well known. The sight of him sent a wave of blatant and subtle hair flipping and primping through the pride of tightly-sheathed girls at the mirrored bar. Within minutes, several flanked him. One of the buff, shirtless, male servers and a friend beckoned Ariel into a spotlight which cast an angelic glow to his blonde hair. He opened the door on his supposed closet, unleashed his femininity and reveled in their adoration of my plastic "Cinderella slippers." He was truly in his element. Nigel and I spotted Karel a few feet away from us. He cut a forlorn figure as he rested his head of golden ringlets against the wall and surveyed the faces flashing in the strobe. Every now and then, he stole a kiss from the Green Fairly in his pocket. Nigel and I decided he was searching for the elusive Anezka.

"Nigel, I think it is cruel of you guys to have made up some fantasy girl for him."

"We did no such thing."

"So you know her, this Anezka?"

"No, she is a friend of one of Mateo's lady friends."

"And yet she never shows up."

"Maybe her keys are stuck to the table," he joked, and I laughed. Nigel rubbed his brow as he did when he fretted, and he glanced again at Karel. "I did once see Mateo speaking to a girl who had those same pink hennaed curls."

"What is so special about her?"

"She is quite pretty and I think she may be Czech."

"Isn't New York is incredible? The whole human race is right here in front of us, Czech, British, Portuguese...I don't know what Ariel is."

"Canadian, I think."

"And the whole rest of the world." Then I pointed to the dance floor, "What's that woman? Caribbean?"

"Could be, or any number of ethnicities. New York is incredible, London too."

"I remember."

He raised his glass to the dance floor, "Hail hail, the gang's all here: Catholics and Jews; rich and poor; educated and not; banker and artist; drunk and sober; sane and…Hey, isn't that the homeless guy who pushes the shopping cart in Times Square?"

"Is he homeless?"

"Maybe not. Things and people are rarely what they seem."

"Yes like the upper reaches in here," he said, and we lifted our eyes toward the crowded balcony. "Careful, you might see more than you bargained for."

"Whatever are you talking about?"

Nigel sidled up to me and all but whispered, "Everyone is having it off up there…"

"Having it off?" Nigel gave a hand-gesture for sex. "Oh! You mean getting it on…Really?! I never knew that."

"It's one of those well-known secrets among certain circles," he said downing his drink.

"Are there private rooms like the Continental Baths in the Ansonia?"

"No. I think that would defeat the whole exhibitionist purpose. Mind you, I have never been up there myself."

A rip tide in the glittered, polyester sea of dancers towed us in. We did not resist at all. The music was so loud it beat out all thoughts from our brains and drowned out the dreaded blue bzzz. It was easy to be with Nigel, who like me, was a terrible dancer. With Val, I had to pay attention and count, be concerned with steps, not a chance of that with Nigel. A few shots of "good whiskey" had rinsed out almost all of his British starch. We threw our arms up in making glad fools of ourselves and reveled with abandon. He free-styled in impressive jig-like steps, spins and squatting Cossack kicks that, in short order, landed him on his butt. Beaming brightly, he reached out for a hand up. The instant our fingers touched, the dancers and dazzling lights blurred, and he came into sharp focus. I had known Nigel since we were undergrads, and he never looked as handsome as he did at that moment. Why? Surely he had always had a square jaw, a mop of silky sandy hair and eyes shining with mischief. He was as attractive as any movie star...*in a blazer, in a comedy*. He leaped up, dropped his hands behind me and pulled me so closely to him that our perspiration-dewed fronts were touching. Steam rose up between us in a fine, hot pheromone-laden mist that cast a shameless spell of attraction over us. We moved in harmonious, unison. He ran his hands along my flanks; I placed my arms around his neck and swayed my hips in playfully, but the spell was broken by a big red flag adorned with Val's face waved in my mind accompanied by the sound of the French woman's words « Allo Oui » and « tire-bouchon ». Abruptly I pushed through the undulating ocean toward the bar, and he grabbed my dress so we would not be separated. We sipped and chatted and visited others we knew from around and the university, and went back to our table where all the Europeans had reconvened. Mateo pointed at a girl and nudged Karel.

"Hey there's Anezka,"

Karel scoffed and disappeared into the crowd.

"Ariel that is unkind. Why do you do that?" I asked.

"He knows we're kidding."

"So there is no girl."

"There is! I met her. She is fabulous!"

The next wave of jet lag almost toppled me over and gave me a good excuse to beg off the rest of the evening. Nigel was ready to go as well, but Ariel slid a small packet of cocaine onto the table and bubbled, "You just need a pick me up."

I passed, but he and Mateo did a line off a girl's overflowing breasts which he then licked clean before kissing her quite passionately, promising to return and walking us to the waiting car. Outside, we gasped and drank in great gobs of the smoke free air. It was magnificently refreshing, and for an instant, all was quiet. Several giggling, über-energetic party goblins snatched Ariel from our midst and dragged him kicking and squealing with in mock protest back into the disco sea. A leggy, pale blonde sheathed in a white mini leaned provocatively against the wall and tossed Mateo a coquettishly seductive glance that prevented him from joining us in the car. "Lenny, take them wherever they want and come back," he told the driver, popped his collar and swaggered to the girl.

Nigel's place was farther uptown by Riverside, so my apartment was the first stop. Through the fluffy layer of snow, he accompanied me to the lobby. Gio was snoring on a cot under a big quilt in his living quarters. Though the lobby was lit, he shined a flashlight on us.

"Hey Doll."

"Hi Gio."

"Whaddya need?"

"Nothing. Thank you."

He waved and went right back to snoring. He only slept over if he had a reason which I told Nigel was the storm that was supposed to be coming. Stifling the attraction between us, we discussed the differences between New York and London; whether or not President Carter should have pardoned the Vietnam draft dodgers and the meaning of love, and then he leaned over me to kiss me, but I pulled away.

"Once, you told me I was a great kisser."

"Once, a million years ago Nigel!"

"It was six. Where were we?"

"Some mixer. We danced barefoot on the lawn in front of the chapel..."

"In light of the full moon."

"You had on a flowing, thing, not that different from this," he said, flicking lightly at my sleeve.

"It's so late Nigel."

"It's almost eight o'clock in the morning in London. Years ago, we never thought about the time," he said at the door and held me tenderly in his arms. "What happened with us?"

"There wasn't really any *us.*"

"There was!"

"Not truly. Or I would never have gone out with Val."

"Damn Val," he joked.

"You're not that cute when you're jealous."

"I know. I did that on purpose, so you don't feel the urge to seduce me."

He always did manage to lighten a heavy situation. I slipped from his arm and saw him out. Once he was gone, I sat by the window reflecting on the past and watching the wind whip the snow-sugared air into hundreds of circles. That whirled in the street lights. The park was buried in snow. Apparently, Gio had been right; a storm was well underway. In the midst of performing my perfunctory bedtime ablutions, I heard foot stomping in front of my door. Through the peephole, I saw Nigel kicking snow from his shoes and shaking it from his hair, so I invited him in. We had neglected to ask the limo driver to wait.

"It's a bloody blizzard. I didn't even see a taxi…"

"Come in." I handed him a towel to dry off, and got out the sheets and blankets for the sofa bed, but he refused any help.

"You're exhausted. Go. I can manage."

In my room, I crawled under my down quilt and fell deep into the mysterious well of sleep. A gentle knocking opened my eyes and I questioned whether I was awake or dreaming. Through a haze in my room, I saw Nigel wearing his shirt and socks. His mouth was moving, but if he was saying anything I couldn't make it out. In my sleep, I mumbled, "Sure. Just don't burn the place down."

✳✳✳

In the bright light of morning, I awakened feeling as if I had been asleep for a very long time. Val was snuggled next to me, so I surmised Nigel had come into the room last night to tell me Val was returning. It was unusually cold, and there was a snow-drift on the floor by the window panes. Large flakes were still coming down. I braced myself to brave the frigid floors and slipped quietly out of bed, so as not to disturb him. Lifting the

Snowy New York Morning ©Winchinchala

edge of the sheet to went to kiss his face, I pulled away. *What?*
"Nigel!?" A smile crept through his lips, and he told me, "Don't
panic love. It's not what you think." He raised the cover to reveal
his fully clothed body.

"Oh please. That doesn't prove anything."

"Trust me. Nothing happened. I would have slept much better."

"There are more blankets in the closet. You…"

"Take it easy. Your answer is in the living room."

Under my extra covers on the sofa bed and the floor there
were the lumpy shapes of sleeping guests. No doubt in a few
hours, I would hear the whole story. I dressed and went downstairs to get some air and an update from Gio. A person was

sacked out in his lounge as well. He was leaning on a shovel bundled up in winter woolies and transfixed on the TV blaring news of the "storm of the century."

"Told you a storm was on the way. Nothing's open Doll. Whaddya need?"

"Just a little air."

"I got plenty," he boasted and opened the door. "I salted the walk, but be careful out there…"

***

I was a lone figure in the middle of Columbus Avenue in the incredible urgency of snow. The street lamps were on and glowed brightly along the avenues like dozens of small, caged stars. Mother Nature had dammed the rush of civilization. The plow had not come through yet, but a couple of cars had gone up 72nd Street to Central Park West allowing me to walk in their tracks to the park. Another had gone before me and left foot-prints that led to the naked Wisteria vines. As Val would have, had he been with me, I cleared a bench and sat watching Nature expressing herself in windy shades of white. I heard the snow-flakes tiny shattering as they landed and doves fluttering to keep dry among the branches but not the fluid blue bzzz. In the dis-tance, a man unleashed his huge Bernese mountain dog who barked his thanks and romped joyfully into the piles of snow which he sent flying in a thousand directions. Oblivious to the elements, he burrowed right down to the ground and then charged across the field beckoning his master to join him in gleeful booming woofs. I watched them until they were out of sight, and then crunched my way back.

The apartment was bustling with the Europeans, and the phone was ringing. Nigel answered before I could. "Hello Val. Yes, this is Nigel. How are you?" I took the phone from him. News of the spectacular storm had reached abroad, and Val was worried. He didn't ask about Nigel, just assured himself that I was "fine," and then I brought up the « tire-bouchon. » I heard his hand hit his forehead. "That was you! You didn't say anything when I called you."

"Neither did you."

"Jerry met a woman in the hall looking for a corkscrew. I didn't have one so we went next door, and she stayed here while we went next door. Why is Nigel there so early?"

"Not Nigel bit all "the Europeans and company are here.""

"Gotta go Babe. Tell me later. Stay warm."

I was eager to find out what had happened myself. Little by little The events of the evening came out. After dropping off Nigel, the driver had returned for Mateo and the rest of the others at 54. When they swung by here for Nigel, the limo got stuck in the deep snow. Nigel had come into my room to ask if they could stay and in my sleep, agreed 'if they didn't burn the place down.' Chuckling, he said, "I think the driver is downstairs with your doorman." Cigarettes were lit while we prepared a "blizzard brunch." Towers of pancakes were warming in the oven. The iron skillet was full of scrambled eggs and we had a platter of raw vegetables and dips. We doubted it would have come together so perfectly if we had planned it a month in advance. Nigel raised his orange juice.

"To our gracious hostess who provided us with such luxurious shelter against the storm."

All replied, "Here here."

With a wry smile, Mateo cut his eyes from me to Nigel and asked, "And how is Val?"

"Missing me in Paris."

Just then a petite cherry red-henna-haired beauty wrapped in a towel slunk into the kitchen.

"Anezka?!"

Karel beamed brightly as he adored her face and opened his arms invitingly to her.

"Everyone this is my Anezka," Karel corrected softly.

149

She giggled coquettishly and slid onto his knee where they exchanged a long, sweet, affectionate kiss.

Titan & Doll

UNITED STATES
MARITIME SERVICE
FOR MERCHANT MARINE SEAMEN
VOLUNTARY ENROLLMENT for SEAGOING MEN
THREE MONTHS TRAINING WITH PAY
ANNUAL TRAINING AND RETAINER PAY
APPLY TO
U.S. MARITIME SERVICE
OR
U.S. COAST GUARD

Titan & Doll

Jackie knew the meaning of hard work. Work was life, and his was aboard a Merchant ship at sea which he had come to consider his home. With a contented heart, he spent much of his time on deck with the salt air in his hair and the weather of the world on his face. Hard-earned experience as a seafarer and his good nature contributed to his success in overseeing the perpetual care of the vessel, the quality of the work and the morale of his crew who performed it. The rich length of his days and nights had carried him to distant shores with a crash of men and laid him merrily tipsy in a patchwork of promiscuous sheets with a delightfully unholy glory of women. His mother often said had been drawn to the sea since the day he was born, and he loved it. When wasn't on it, he was often watching it from the waterfront noting the incredible patterns created by a breeze or a gust of wind. In them he heard stories, the echoes of people's voices from as faraway as old King Herod's Palace and as new as Manhattan's Chelsea Piers between 12th and 23rd Streets. "Lots of terrible things happened in them places," Jackie told people. "The Titanic had been expected but never sailed into Pier 54. And that big fire. You know the pier by the National Biscuit Company...Man those big black smoke clouds billowed into the air for two days. Two days! More than a hundred firemen came close to death trying to fight that blazing beast; New York Fire Department's a tough bunch. Thank God they Romans at Herod's. way back in the B.C. times didn't have that fire department. Jews setting that palace on fire, while they were inside, saved them from a fate worst than death. How's that for a grisly damn truth? The Romans must have had a rabid, dog-dirty deed planned to make them do that."

He swore to his friends that the sea churned and tossed the cries of victims and the sighs of lovers for all eternity, so their pain and passion would never be forgotten. In every port where there were ancient ruins, he would verify the tales of love and death about which he had heard or read by visiting the "scenes of the crime," as he called them, and he engaged in his own love stories. While he was too shy around women to wolf after companionship, he never spent a shore leave alone. The prevailing theory among his friends was that he was just one of those men who's "got it," and that included his attractive height which was formed by his long legs and big torso squared off with broad shoulders.

"I mean jeez, how tall are you Jackie, 6' 4?" Seamus asked.

Lucky Lou. Replied, "Yeah, that's without a cap, and chicks love your square jaw and…"

Bird Man cut in, "and get this…I heard a broad tell another she liked your shoulders, said, 'I have someplace to put my feet.'"

Jackie burst out laughing and denied their claims. ""It's not how I look. I'm just open to all women. A choosy man is a lonely man. I'll even do loony." He chortled and continued softly, "Maybe I won't do stupid, take advantage…well, unless there's absolutely no one else."

Indeed, life had provided a pageant of women from which he could choose,, every size, shape, color and temperament: waitresses in aprons; ladies in furs; island girls in leis; Asian dolls in dresses slit up to their fortune cookies and on and on around the world. He separated them into day and night. His day-girls were sweet, possessed of an almost palpable vulnerability. Their tender hearts overflowed with nurturing kindness and their heads with pastel fairy tales of the pure loves they had but lost to the war or other unfortunate circumstance. They often became martyrs and enjoyed the position's attendant sympathy and respect, so it was in the guise of accepting his help around the house they sought his company. They seemed compelled to convince him they were "not that kind of girl," one who picks up or is picked up by men. Yet once he was in their homes and they were in his arms, the sugar from which they were made melted on the hot iron skillet of his manliness. By morning, their pillows were invariably under his head and their bodies tucked by his torso. Night-girls were impertinent, racy, and callous. They were the scorned and the promiscuous, slumming debutantes; the career barmaids; the too-tipsy hussies or the outcasts who Jackie mashed. Being perceived as desirable and spinning their sugar into the fluffy fun of perishable cotton candy was the obvious name of their game. Tingling first night flirtations fast became last nights by dawn, so they could walk away physically satisfied and emotionally untouched. Girls, by day or by night, were available for a dash of his poetic flattery, intense attention or wide, sturdy shoulders. Each was a land unto herself, that as he did with the ancient ruins, he explored wholeheartedly. In slaking his desires, he felt as if he was combating the tragic pandemic caused by loneliness in the world. That mission, the ports with their culture and history and the life aboard ship were his reasons for worshipping life on the ocean. He felt he was one with it. Jackie didn't lay any claim to being from any place in particular, but he did go ashore every now and then to a place he called "home."

***

`The Salty Dog on the corner of Ocean Avenue. The pub faced a window that stretched from one end of the wall to the other; it provided the patrons a view of the harbor, boats coming and going and who was doing what where. Once, in 1953, Seamus O'Reilly, the owner toyed with a new interior design which would have replaced the window with a wall and paintings of the sea. The Dog, as the regulars called it, was really cold in the winter, and Seamus thought blocking off the window would help keep the place warm in the biting cold winter months. It was the talk of the bar for weeks. Everyone wondered if anyone had ever complained about being cold. No one had, and no one approved of the plan except Seamus and Michaela, the interior designer he had consulted. She had refined features, a head of thick, permed curls and a long slim waist beneath, "a couple of luscious honeydews," Lucky-Lou noted with a naughty grin. In fact, the patrons thought Seamus' fondness for melons might have contributed to his decision to hire her. "Who wastes money on waterfront property then blocks it off?" became an often repeated phrase among the regulars. A few of them even called the Michaela over to their area one day, offered her a drink and then their opinion. They came to the Salty Dog to look outside, see the boats. With self-righteousness, thinly veiled in charm, she dismissed them. "Now come on boys. Just try it. If you want to see the boats you can step outside." They had a meeting among themselves and nominated Jackie to present the counter-argument again. To that end, he advised them to go the bar across the way which they didn't like because it had pretzels not nuts, but as always, they did what Jackie asked. A mutual attraction between Jackie and Michaela cause the debate to go long, but in the end they arrived at a solution that would make everyone happy. She proposed hanging a heavy canvas curtain that could be raised on warm days. Jackie lit up and said, "Like a sail. What a great idea!" From then on his cronies announced his presence with, "There he is... the savior of the ocean!"

Though not formally educated, Jackie was the smartest of the bunch down at the Salty Dog. Anytime questions came up someone would inevitably suggest, "Go ask Jackie." He usually knew the answer. At the age of forty-two, experience had taught him a good deal; the rest he attributed to reading. "I read a lot. My fo'c'sle is full of books. And when I'm not aboard, I read the paper everyday. Shit, sometimes I read it twice. A person's gotta read," he told them and advised anyone who asked him about how he knew so much. Then he'd reach into his jacket and pull out a book. He always had one with him. They were books on a wide variety of topics; history, archaeology, animals, short stories, not because his interests were so varied but because those were the books by the plate glass window of Bird Man's, the local bookstore. He bought reading materials on Thursday when the shop was open late, so everyone could see him. He would position himself, book in hand, weighing it, examining it, and patiently standing until an expected tap on the glass arrived from one of his buddies on the way to the Salty Dog. He'd wait for him to tap a second time, and then, look up as if the sound had snatched him from deep thought. He'd smile and give a little wave. No one ever came in after him. Everyone knew he'd arrive later maybe show them the book or provide a tasty tidbit he had read to fill in the lulls in their conversations. "Today I read that a regular Joe is mostly water, like sixty percent. Now there ain't no numbers to back this up yet, but I probably got much more, and that's why I like the sea. I am the sea." Or "You know, "Cockroaches are the oldest livin' creatures on earth?" or "Japanese people speak Russian in part of Japan," or "We gotta have war, so'z we can have peace," sparked interest and to his amusement often ignited loud arguments. Quietly he'd sit and sip his beer as the liquor-laced logic spun around the group.

Once, he struck up the blaze with, "Hey, today I read pigs are super smart, actually smarter than dogs."

"If pigs are so smart, how come I'm eatin' em for breakfast?" Lucky Lou asked.

"Ha! If you're eatin' so much pig, how come you ain't smarter?" Bird Man shot back.

"What the fuck kind o' dumb ass question is that?"

"What? You never heard that expression, 'You are what you eat'?"

"All I know is this morning, I heard you say, "I don't know how I can eat this shit," so what's that say about you hot shot?"

"Aw shut up."

"Pigs have to be smarter," Smitty butt in with conviction.

"Why?" asked all in a chorus.

"It means they get eat cuz they like to get eaten. And me, myself, I love to get eaten," he grinned and slurped his beer as the others continued until they turned to Jackie. He cleverly switched topics.

"What's more is, pigs don't even sweat. Sweat like a pig. Who made that up? A horse sweats the most, right?"

No one knew that to be a fact or any of the other points he brought up, but no one ever argued with Jackie. His insecurity about his intelligence interfered with his ability to be a good listener, and he would become obstinate. If he was proven wrong, or as he said, "made a fool of," his temper would burn in his face, and he would lash out with his booming voice. Rage was one of his shortcomings, the other was jealousy. If anyone checked out a girl he was dating, had dated or considering, impulse would peel reason away to reveal his legendary temper. His body took over, and he'd express himself with his fist making repeated contact with doors, tables, chairs or the unfortunate person who either dared to confront him or neglected to stand back. For that reason and the manly code of mutual respect, they steered clear of women around him until his pick was clear. So if they saw a one at the Salty Dog they wanted to ask out, they spoke up right away to stake their claims before Jackie even saw her. Five years ago, that all changed; they could take their time and had their pick because Jackie had lost interest in a new girl. Alida had come into his life.

***

"That Alida, she's got Jackie by the balls," Lucky Lou said every time Jackie was running late. If Jackie heard him, he made the same correction, "No! No, she don't. Doll's got me by my heart and soul." His sense of self had sky-rocketed when she came into his life. It was about the same time he saved the ocean view at the Dog. One October Thursday, he first saw her in Bird Man's Books. Though he guessed she was in her early thirties, she possessed the angelic allure. She had dressed her lips in creamy scarlet and her long, soft brown hair hung down to her generous shapely hips.

Her peachy complexion and perfectly round azure irises reminded him of a doll he had seen in an antique store in France. Her paperweight eyes opened when he picked her up and mesmerized him, for in those scintillating glass spheres, he saw life, life as if the doll possessed a spirit. He adjusted her long scarf that was the most uniquely vivid shade of blue he had ever seen before. When he fluffed up her dress, the hem stuck on his button and revealed her undergarments; he immediately smoothed it back down. Upon righting the doll, her face flushed crimson, and he almost dropped her. She felt warm to his touch. *That's impossible,* he told himself. In scrutinizing her more closely, he attracted the shopkeeper. "Est-ce que je peux vous aider, monsieur?" With the little French he had learned from visits to Le Havre, he replied, "Elle est rougit quand je... you know, when I lifted sa robe." In an attempt to reproduce the effect, he turned the doll upside down again, but the doll remained the same color. The shopkeeper could not make sense of what he was saying, politely smiled and attended to another customer. Tipping the doll a third time, she turned red again. He checked to see if anyone else had witnessed her change color, but there was no one nearby. He questioned his own sanity, but for more than an hour, he held her while he feigned interest in other objects. As a bachelor with no family and no steady girl he was too embarrassed to buy her. He settled on a trinket and carefully sat the doll on a blanket. Voyages to Le Havre always began with a visit to her. His fascination with the doll encouraged the shopkeeper to take better care of her than she had previously. She displayed her on a pillow. To their mutual surprise, on his last visit, the doll was no where to be found, though the shopkeeper had not sold it. Together they hunted around and behind and under every spot where she could have fallen. "La poupée doit avoir été vole." Jackie decided the theft was fate interrupting his obsession, so he could focus on finding a real live doll.

And there she was, in person in front of Bird Man who was gushing over her, taking a very long time to do ring up her purchase. Jackie didn't care; he knew Bird couldn't score a broad like that. He had a beak nose and spit a little bit when he spoke, shortcomings not offset by any great brains or charm. He didn't even know that much about books. He had inherited the place, which was named after him, when his father died three years ago. Then everyone started calling him by his full name, Bird Man instead of just Bird. Knowing that he posed no threat, Jackie calmly pondered what to say to her. As he stepped in, the shop bell jingled.

"Hey, Bird Man," he called out rubbing his hands together.

"Hey Jackie."

The woman glanced over and a magnet of attraction drew their eyes together. For the longest time, neither could look away. Shyly she smiled and stroked the book in her hand. He took advantage of Bird Man's being busy with another customer to talk to her. *Oresteia* was embossed in gold on the cover of the book she was holding. He had no idea how to pronounce the Greek word he had seen in his mandatory Greek class at school. For a split-second he hated himself for having ditched it. He knew she spoke English because he heard her talking to Bird Man, but her resemblance to the doll, and his desire to impress her forced out, "Parlez vous anglais?" With a disarmingly musical laugh she replied. "Bien sûr, et un peu de Français." The way she tossed her hair and fixed her glittering eyes on his, sent a wave of exciting erotic energy through his body. "Et vous monsieur?" He put his hand to his chest, and inhaled deeply to calm himself before he spoke, "Yeah. I'm American." Bird Man called out from the back of the store and stole her attention. "Miss, Is this the other book?" He waved it up in the air. When she placed *Oresteia* on the counter and walked toward him, Jackie skimmed the blurb on the back that, to his relief, was in English, not Greek as he feared. Bird Man apologized to her because the volume he had found was not the one she wanted and advised her that he could order it and "have it in about three weeks." Jackie stood off to the side of the door making a mental note of the date she was supposed to return.

"Oh, don't forget your book," Jackie said handing the *Oresteia* to her.

"Thank you."

Neither said anything else a long minute. With flirtatious deliberation, she sized him up.

"Have you read the *Oresteia*?"

"That?" he asked tapping the cover. "Yeah, sure," he announced so proudly, she pulled her head back with surprise and skepticism. Sheepishly, he downplayed his false claim, "I mean it's been a while." With a few random words from the back, he cobbled together a reply. "But it's, you know, a real lyric tragedy, all the revenge and hating and cutting people into bits for bird food."

"Oh really?"

"I guess you know more about it than I do."

"I wouldn't be so sure."

He looked at the author's name, "Aeschylus. Greek writer, philo--ophilos, hate-in-love."

"Oh you know French and Greek?"

"I know a Greek guy, so Miló polý líga elliniká," he indicated very little with his thumb and index finger.

The sound of her voice was so lovely and musical that he stared at her and wondered if she made such beautiful sounds when she made love.

"Maybe we could talk about the..."

"*Oresteia* when you get back?" she guessed.

"How did you know I was going anywhere?"

Her eyes fell on the lanyard around his neck. "I've never seen such fine weaving on such a slim rope," she observed lifting it from his sweater for a closer look. Her nails scratched his chest and sent a tingle through his body. "So intricate. Wherever did you get it?"

Her face was almost touching the sweater, the top of her head was right under his nose. He breathed in her hair, and instantly recognized jasmine.

"I made it."

Impressed but dubious, she turned her eyes upward to his, "Really?"

"Yeah. I didn't like the one that came with it, so I made this one."

"What was wrong with the original?"

"It got all twisted going in and out of my pocket. Gotta have more strands so it's heavy enough to lay down flat, look nice...."

"Beautiful. Do I have to be a seaman to get one?" Her fingers ran down the ridges of the braid to the end. "And this whistle...?"

"No. It's not a whistle. It's a pipe, a Bosun's pipe."

"A Bosun's pipe. I see." She placed it in his breast pocket and gave it a little pat, "Very attractive, indeed."

The tingling continued to ebb and flow beneath his skin. As she headed toward the door, he took a giant step in front of her to get there first.

"I'm expecting the book I ordered in a few weeks. Maybe then?"

"Maybe."

As she exited, Jackie was again reminded of the French doll

because a sudden autumn zephyr tossed up her hair and the hem of her skirt. Bird Man watched her too.

"What a Goddamn living doll," Jackie said.

"You can say that again. She even moves like one."

"What's that supposed to mean?"

"I dunno, like a lady. Bet she won't turn around,"

"Sure she will. She's swaying her hips for me."

"Two bucks says she don't."

"You're on Bird Man."

Jackie held out his hand for Bird to pay as he drew nearer to the window. Once she was across the street without looking back, Bird held out his hand.

"Ha. Pay up Jack..."

But before he could finish, the doll shot her eyes over her shoulder. Bird slapped down two bills and Jackie waved a little good-bye to the woman. Before rounding the corner, she did it again.

Jackie slapped his hands together, "And that was a double take!"

"Say Jackie, I have known you for how long? I never saw you read Aeschylus."

"You ever been on board a ship with me for six months?" There was no response in the three seconds he waited. "Then shut up.

"I'd read it too if it would put me in the runnin' for her..."

"Yeah, but you're not 'in the running for her' you son of a bitch!"

Jackie reached over the counter and grabbed Bird Man's shirt with a powerful force that tore it.

"Shit! Jackie! Let me go! I was just talking."

He let him go, straightened out his clothes, raised his arms and mustered a smile for the two customers in the store.

"Just a friendly disagreement. Nothing to see."

His temper slammed him out of the shop to find a different store and prevent Bird Man from discovering he hadn't actually read it. His latest assignment put him aboard a ship bound for the Far East that would provide plenty of time to study the book before he saw her again. *Her?* He muttered a loud. He couldn't believe it. He hadn't even asked the doll her name. At the third book store, he still had no copy of *Oresteia*, and the clerk directed him to the public library. Jackie laughed to himself.

The library had long served as a refuge to him when he wanted to be alone with his thoughts. He was fascinated by books, people spilling their thoughts onto pages and communicating through time, imparting their knowledge, telling stories of worlds around them and in their heads. He was thankful to their authors for what they taught him and making him appear better educated than he was. From the time he was quite young, he would plop down in a big, hard wooden chair and read. He never imagined skirt chasing would place him in the library, but it did. He got the book. He felt good walking around with the big volume. On his way to check it out, he heard what he thought was the woman's musical laughter. It was. She was one of the librarians.

"Hi," she peeled and waved walking toward him. "What are you doing here?" She giggled and answered herself. "I guess you're getting a book."

Before he could protest, she had taken it from him.

Uncharacteristically nervous, he shuffled nervously and whispered, "Yeah. You know, seeing it today made me want to reread some stuff, and um, well, my copy is lent out. You know how people are."

"Yes, I do know," she said sweetly and returned the book. He held her finger and she raised her eyes to his in an enduring gaze. An unseen magnet held them in a still captive silence.

"If you've already read it, I would be at a disadvantage."

"Probably not."

"Shall we have a challenge instead?"

"What kind of a challenge?"

"Let's see who finishes it first, Okay?"

"Yeah, I'm shipping out to Bombay, so..."

Bombay?! That far? You'll be gone for months," she said and lowered her head in disappointment.

"That's the way it is with Merchant...."

"Yes, but well we just met, and..."

He sensed he was about to lose her and tried to get her to hang on.

"It won't seem long. I'll write. Okay? I will. I promise." When she didn't answer, he asked, "Okay?" a second time and lifted her chin with his finger.

"Oh, a seaman who writes?"

"Writes and reads! That's me," he boasted and ran his palm over his chest.

A patron needed her help; so he quickly wrote down her name and address.

Alida?

"My mother picked it. Latin, for small winged one or something."

"Maybe angel."

"Let's hope not, for your sake," she declared with a naughty wink.

The old woman at circulation was surprised to see the manly seaman checking out the Greek text. He announced that he and "Alida, the librarian," were reading it.

"Isn't that lovely, pursuing knowledge in the name of love?"

✳✳✳

He never had to call Alida. The letters he had sent from exotic ports were so charming and intriguing that she could hardly wait to see their author again. Upon seeing him on the deck, she waved eagerly and jumped up and down. The sight cracked his weathered face into a grin.

"Alida! Ahoy! Alida!"

He threw down his duffle bag down and drew her into the

warmth of his coat for a long embrace.

And then she surprised him by saying, "I'm almost sorry to see you."

"What?"

His downcast expression hurried her explanation, "Your letters are divine, extraordinary."

"You really think so?"

Stretching on tip toe, she kissed him.

"Here, I brung you something Doll."

Alida unwrapped the golden bangle and slid onto her small wrist. "I love it."

She threw him the keys to her Chevy, and they drove to the shore, bundled up and walked along the cool, deserted winter beach. Her desire to go directly to the sea instantly deepened his feelings for her.

"You should see the sea in Greece. Blue, blue blue. Kinda like your...."

"What's wrong?"

She was wrapping a long blue scar around her neck.

"Where did you get that?"

"My great grandmother. She bought it...

"Don't tell me. In France..."

"Good guess," she said with a laugh.

He took her hand and they walked along the beach until they were forced into one another's arms by the damp, biting, sea breeze.

"I love the ocean," he declared taking a mighty breath.

"I can see why?"

"He's one of my best friends."

"You mean she?"

"No. The Ocean is definitely a man. A woman could never be that powerful."

"There are Titans who are..."

"Well, I am more mortal. That's why I can't beat him. No one can. Ocean reminds us little humans that we aren't in charge of anything.

"That's why you are so fond of him?"

"That and he's taken me all over the world, kept me company on a lot of lonely beaches."

She studied his face as he stared at the sea. Suddenly he picked her up; she squealed and kicked gleefully. As soon as her soles touched the earth again, she raced him to the car in a flurry of sand and mirth. They closed the windows and turned up the heat and got under one another and rocked the car, to rolling down a small hill. They didn't even know it until they had finished and were catching their breath. Jackie jumped half naked out of the back, into the front seat and jammed on the brake. They dissolved into laughter.

Once they recovered, she asked, "So Jackie, what did you think?"

"You are fabulous, we got a real connection. I will be seeing you a lot!"

"About the book, *Oresteia?*" she clarified and waited, but he didn't answer. She gasped in disbelief and slapped him playfully. "You did not read it."

"I couldn't," he replied defensively.

"Why not?"

"That book I checked out? It was in Greek. I thought I had the translation."

"Awww. Don't feel lousy. I didn't read it either."

They giggled and guffawed, and in that moment of shared merriment, he recognized that she had him by all that was holy and all that was not. He started to tickle her, and she escaped by getting out. Pantsless, he sprang after her letting all that was not holy flop freely. He was amazed he had caught the bright, warm, brilliant Alida.

For months, the fire they lit on the beach that night burned steadily and grew brighter. She called him her Titan, and he called her Doll. When they were together, the stars shined in the day time and the sun at night. Time stood still and time slipped away. He found the mettle to finally divorce his first wife whom he hadn't seen for nearly a decade and had no desire to see, in order to marry his doll, Alida. No matter when his ship came in, his wife, was waiting for him. For each voyage, she saw him off with a new book. It became their thing. They talked about them, and read them aloud, and while they had read many, they always came back to the Greeks.

Aeschylus was Jackie's favorite author because his fantastic tales of history and Gods and chariots leaped to life for him. One star-filled night in the Mediterranean, "I saw that chorus of winged nymphs traveling through the sky in a chariot with my own eyes. What an imagination he had! And he got it right."

"Got what right?"

"He didn't say the great Titan, Oceanus was Prometheus' sister. Oceanus was his brother. Obviously Doll, the ocean's a man."

"Yes, a man who was married to his sister," she added.

"Tethys was his sister. I guess the Titans had to choose among their own when it came to broads...but a sister? That would never be for me. No God damn way. I'd be a monk or beg to be a mortal..." he grabbed her tightly around her waist and kissed her, "I would choose you over mortality any day Doll."

"I would be waiting."

When they weren't reading, they whiled away the hours languishing in closeness. To her delight, he regaled her with first hand accounts of the far flung corners of the world which she knew she "would not have the opportunity to see, at least not in this life time." Once in a while, the countries' histories he recounted were quite violent and she would cover her ears and repeat, "La la la."

"Okay. Sorry Doll. That's one for the boys down at the Dog, not you. How about a love story?" Any story he told was guaranteed to entertain her because he was incredibly skilled at making the character's voices and mannerisms, including the girls.

"Crazy Love"

"It's important to remember, this is a for real story."

"Oh, a true story. I love true stories."

"Okay Doll, come with me for a little time travel and head for the 18th century out on an island in the middle of the Pacific; although, it doesn't really matter when we get there. A tropical paradise is always a tropical paradise. It's what you call lush with palms swaying in the air full of plumeria and jasmine; there are bright orange and white striped fish gliding through water, light blue here, turquoise there, dark in the middle. The beach is white sand, pure white, soft like confectionary sugar. Gorgeous and peaceful. Suddenly, a girl comes, running and giggling, all arms and limbs, no top on, so her island pleasures are bouncing on her chest. She's running from a young, island buck, right behind her, handsome son of a gun. Big. And all over, you know?"

He grabs the wooden pepper mill and holds it straight out from his crotch, and Alida blushed and laughed into her hand.

"Oh grinding love."

"I am surprised a cute doll like you knows about that. Anyways, so there they are, their teeth filling up their faces with happiness. A couple of clouds drift in front of the sun and dim the day. Together they say, 'Taya' mina'lak sin hinemhum.' I heard it means there is no brightness without the darkness. They go on with their flirting. The wind is streaming their long, black hair behind them. The skies and everything are grey, but not around them. They radiate that," he snaps his fingers to recall a word, "aura, that sunny glow you see around soulful people and star-crossed lovers."

Jackie got a little nervous. He knew well that there were countless stories of tragic love that had been told and retold, and Alida had probably read them all. He felt pressured to add small details and deliver it with more than usual theatrical flair.

"Inina, the girl, is from a local family, not too much dough and they have four daughters. This one is a real knock out.

Inapo, the boy, really loves her, so he goes to his family and says he wants to marry her. She's the one. To his face, his mother argues, 'Inina? No Inapo. No dowry. And she's too pretty. The pretty ones never want to do their share of work.' His father agrees and asks him what is wrong with his cousin, Tadtasi. Inapo blows up. 'I don't love her, and one of her eyes doesn't open all the way. That's what's wrong with her. You don't understand,' and he storms off. Behind his back, his parents laugh at how upset he is cuz they're just teasing him. In the meantime, along comes the new Spanish Captain, takes one look at Inina, and he wants to marry her too. He's been to enough islands to be wise in the ways of their courtship. He puts on his dress uniform with the fluffy tassels and brass buttons to present himself to the father. 'That's kind of you Mr. Captain, but there is no dowry,' he tells him. The captain is shocked. 'You gonna pay me?! Your daughter is so beautiful, I will pay you.' He clapped his hands and his crew dragged in a trunk full of small mirrors, dishes, cooking pots large enough for an entire goat's head and bolts of fabric. It was a whole lot of nothing' that looks like something if you don't have much and you never saw it before and…"

Jackie reached in his pocket and threw out a handful of coins that banged on the coffee table with a jingling clatter.

"And of course there was silver and gold, not much to the captain but it was a lot to the father. It could be a dowry for his two younger daughters. Across the room his wife is waving off the deal. Little tears run down her face. The father goes to her. In his ear she tells him, 'I got enough pots. What about Inapo and Inina? They are in love.' Her voice tugs at his heart, but not his business sense. He shakes the captain's hand. Later on he explains the logic to the Missus. 'Inina has to suffer marrying the captain, not so old, not that bad looking. She can endure being rich, so her sisters might get good husbands too.' The wife is not pleased, but she accepts what he says because she is an island wife, but she does insist he tell Inina. When he does, he speaks very softly. Inina shakes her head back and forth, but he talks and talks and talks. He uses words that she has to listen to such as honor, obedience and respect. By the time he finishes, she is nodding. That night she tiptoes to Inapo."

Jackie taps on the pepper mill and winks.

"The next day when the captain shows up? Inina is gone."

Alida was spellbound.

"So Inina is gone. The captain shouts '¿Qué? You have my money. ¿Donde está mi novia. Bring her or, I gonna kill you!'"

Jackie demonstrates by grabbing her gently by her soft throat.

"To save their father, when the sisters spot Inina, they tattle, 'We saw them on the beach!'"

Jackie holds up his fingers to count off.

"The father, the captain, Inapo's parents, the soldiers; the whole village heads over. All morning they go in the caves, beat the bushes, even shake the cocoanut trees, but they don't see them. The captain smells a wild goose and draws his sword, but one of the sisters yells, 'Up there!' All eyes turn to the cliff. There they stood, Inina and Inapo sharing a kiss. That aura was shining like a huge diamond halo over their heads. They had woven their hair together in a fat braid that hung right in the middle of them. 'Inina!!' her father cries, but he was too late. She and Inapo jump. And right there in front of the whole village and their mothers and the midwives who brought 'em into the world, they left."

To create the sound of their bodies hitting the ground, Jackie dropped himself down hard on one knee.

Wide-eyed Alida gasped.

"And then silence. For a whole minute," he whispered, "nothing moved. No birds. No wind. No waves. The ocean was perfectly still, just a mirror full of grey sky."

Slowly he rose to his feet with his Bo'sun's call in his mouth piping *The Still,* used to demand silence on the ship. He played it for a full seven seconds.

"And you know what? They never found those kids' bodies."

"They washed out to sea?"

"No. Whatever falls there stays, but not them. But over the years, anybody who went to the spot swore Inapo and Inina had become ghosts. They heard their voices, and not just the locals, visitors from faraway places who didn't know about Inapo and Inina."

"How did they know it was them, not just the wind?"

"The reports were always the same, 'We heard two young people laughing,' and in particular, the words, 'Taya' mina'lak sin hinemhum." At first the village thought the two lovers were hiding, somehow living in the caves. Even after they would have been too old to still be alive, people heard them. Decades later, one of the new mayors decided to settle the mystery once and for all, and he sent a crew to investigate. You know what they found?"

"Oh dear. Is this icky and violent?"

"No, nothing like that. It's amazing. They found Inapo and Inina."

"Alive?!"

"Fossils. They were lying right next to each other covered in limestone."

Shaking her head in disbelief, she told him, "You said this was a true story."

"It is. I saw them with my own eyes. Wait."

He leaped up and retrieved his box of photos from a shelf, snapped one out and presented it to her. The power of the image morphed her doubt into astonishment. Tipping her head, she analyzed the two human forms.

More softly than usual, she remarked, "they're holding hands, and...is their hair braided together?"

"I took that picture through the water and couldn't get a clearer shot, but that's what I thought too."

Moved by the touching proof of the young lovers' love fossilized for all eternity, she threw her arms around Jackie and wept.

"So beautiful and so sad, that is crazy love."

For as much as she loved his stories, he loved her home-cooked meals. Together they ate and laughed and lived in their house on Ocean Avenue in a cozy web spun from the invisible strands of contented love and comfortable monotony.

***

For the upcoming trip, Alida gave Jackie a copy of Ferling-hetti's *A Coney Island of the Mind.* a poem. On the ship, he had to fight to read it in peace after a misunderstanding with his shipmate, Sven, a lighthearted seaman from Sweden.

"Poetry. Poetry is for pussar," Sven said in his usual booming voice.

"Pussar? Like pussy. You calling me a pussy?!"

Jackie didn't wait for a reply. He snatched his book and squashed Sven against the metal door and held him there with his body. "Listen you dumb Swede!" he demanded and read a loud, "'I am the man.' Does that sound like pussy readin' to you? 'I was there. I suffered, somewhat. I am an American. I have a passport.' Are you listening to me?" He asked choking Sven until he agreed, then he ordered him to sit down. Sven obeyed cheer-fully and lay back with his arms behind his head. Jackie opened the nine page poem and didn't stop until he had spoken every word. Sven nodded at some phrases and at the end applauded.

"Mycket bra."

From the clapping Jackie figured he liked it and said, "All right then."

"I förbigående så pass uttrycka medel kyss."

"What?

"Pussor is not pussies. It means kisses. Girls like men who read poetry. It doesn't mean the other thing Yackie.

"Oh yeah?

"Yeah."

"So how do you say the other?"

"Fitta."

"Fitta? I like pussy better," he said and laughed off the dis-agreement with Sven. "You pack a good punch man."

"You too, Yackie," he admitted rubbing his face.

They shook hands.

***

The ship returned a day early, and Jackie couldn't wait to see Doll, hold her in his arms, and lose his face in her sea of wavy hair. Winter trounced across the pier, but the book in his coat pocket kept him warm. The florist began arranging a bouquet as soon as she saw Jackie, and the waiter at the Chinese restaurant dropped in a serving of the "extra special sauce for your lady." Anticipation hustled Jackie home, but Alida was not there. The only movement was a draft slicing in from the kitchen window. The house was quite cold, and from the snow that had drifted on the floor by the window; he guessed she hadn't been there for some time. The kitchen faucet dripped and dripped and dripped. The clock ticked and ticked and ticked, yet time seemed to stand in the house made colder by Alida's absence. Its flaws, the rip in the curtain, cigarette burns on the couch and the wear on the path in the rug leaped out at him beneath an ubiquitous grey haze. He donned her bright blue scarf that was left dangling on a chair, toyed with the end and tried to locate her by calling her friends. Mimi told him the storm had knocked out the electricity in his neighborhood.

"A couple of days ago, so I invited Alida to stay here."

The lamp lit when he flicked the switch. "It's back on now. Put her on the phone."

"Well I can't Jackie. Lowell took her ..."

"Lowell?! Lowell Hunter? He's there?"

"Not now silly. He's out with Alida to pick up a few albums for our winter party. You're invited of course."

He forced out a laugh and a thank you. Mention of Lowell ignited the unfound suspicion and distrust in his possessive macho soul. Other than Jackie himself, no one doubted Alida's love and devotion to him. He snatched up a photo from last New Year's Eve in which Alida leaned with the charming, aristocrat Lowell Hunter on his new Mercedes Roadster. The women in their circle defined the bachelor as "swanky" or "dreamy" like "that actor Cary Grant" and cunningly vied for his attention, not Alida. She summed him up as "bo-ri-ing and conceited" and "not likely to pick any of you. He's just slumming," she concluded after having "endured a couple of dates with him." That knowledge aroused the envy that gnawed at Jackie when he saw them in the photo or in person as he did the night it was taken.

Usually she dressed in prim white blouses and tweed and shined with the vulnerable sweetness of a girl-next-door librarian, but for the holiday party, she had zipped herself into a screaming, figure-hugging, holiday-red dress and became a beguiling enchantress. During the party, whenever Alida's back was to Lowell, he ogled the qualities nature had given her. Once, their eyes met when they both reached for the cigarette lighter on the table. He hung an alluring smile on the corner of his mouth, but she was so oblivious to his existence, she missed it. Witnessing Lowell's failed gesture, Jackie let let out an amused chuckle. She heard him and beamed a broad, open smile to her strong Titan that made him feel as his feet had lifted off the floor. He was very proud of her and when people asked what she did, he urged her to, "Tell 'em what you do Doll. Go on," and when she told them, "I'm a librarian," no one ever believed. "I've got two women. They know each other and they both love me," he boasted.

Damn it! Where are you? Snow storm, he mumbled to himself and jammed his thumb into Lowell's face in the photo. *Son of a bitch. I better not find out you been sneaking around here.* He tossed the photo down and then caught sight of himself in the mirror over the mantle. Reflected there was a man he feared, one he never wanted to meet, an old man, and the longer he looked, the older he got, the uglier he made himself out to be, an ancient mariner, with little more than a ditty bag, and an armful of books whose ineloquent speech flaunted his lack of formal education, whose life ebbed and flowed with the will of his master, his brother, the sea. A stormy ball of self-doubt and anger rolled up inside of him which he fought to control and eliminate before Alida returned. She abhorred his temper, which she made abundantly clear the first time he lost his in front of her in an Italian restaurant.

When the waiter brought the Macaroni Alla Carbonara Jackie had ordered, he politely suggested it was not his "macaroni" because the dish was full of spaghetti.

The waiter flashed a grin and explained in his thick, native Italian accent, "Sì. Is Macaroni Alla Carbonara signore."

Jackie lifted a few long noodles on his fork and asked, "This look like macaroni?"

"Sì. Sì, lo fa perché è maccheroni," he replied in sharp, loud tones that attracted other diners as well as the Maitre' D who confronted the waiter and engaged him in an animated discussion.

Embarrassed, Alida hid her face in her glove.

Jackie attempted to interrupt, "Hey! Hey! "I came here for a nice dinner with my girl, and..." Their own argument in Italian had superseded the waiter's with Jackie. Exasperated, he announced to Alida, "Come on Doll. Let's get out of here.!"

Simultaneously, she wanted to leave and stay because she wanted to pay for the antipasto and wine they had already consumed, but as soon as he pulled out her chair, she got up and left with him. For a good portion of the walk home, he blew off the majority of steam about "how that idiot brought spaghetti instead of macaroni," before he realized Alida hadn't spoken, not one word. Her reticence spilled over into the next day and the next. His ham-handed attempts at coaxing conversation from her failed. "What's a matter doll? Great ox standing on your tongue or something?" His *Oreistia* reference did not loosen her tongue. Time did and Sunday at breakfast, she spoke.

"Jackie…" she began timidly.

He searched the air and grinned, "Where is that beautiful voice coming from?"

By then the incident had slipped his mind.

"In the restaurant."

"Oh yeah the spaghetti instead of the macaroni. That meat head…"

"Well Jackie. See, it's all macaroni to an Italian."

"Macaroni is macaroni and spaghetti is sp…"

"In English. In Italian, Macaroni means pasta. Had you not been such a hot head and such a wrong hot head, I…"

"Hot head?"

"Yes. Who can talk to you when you are so angry?"

"Ha. So you been giving me the silent treatment all this time because of that."

"Yes, until you cooled down."

"Oh, like Aeschylus said, 'a sick mind may be cured by words if the time's right. But when that mind is still infected with rage, you can't force the swelling down.'"

"The first time you read those words in *Prometheus Bound* you said…"

"Amen to that. I remember Doll. Listen, I said I was sorry. I am. I'll do better Alida. I'm a Titan, right?"

"More of a barbarian I'd say, and I don't want to be with a barbarian Jackie."

She turned and floated away from him like a gentle inlet returning to the sea.

Alida reverberated in his head with the fear that she had dumped him; she who the boys at the Dog adored and who somehow convinced her uptown friends Jackie was "brilliant." Because of her, he ate fine cuisine at upscale restaurants and knew which of the many forks to use for what. He attended the opera and theatre and, as he told his cronies, "understood everything." Because of her, books whet his appetite for discussions, and he learned to be as astute and inquisitive listener as she was.

177

When she encouraged him to do what she couldn't, "take the writers home, and get a different vantage point yourself," he carried Hesse to Germany; Guillen to Cuba, and Aeschylus to Greece. In Athens, he talked Sven into taking a taxi 14 miles to Aeschylus' birthplace, Eleusis. Jackie stood in the spot where he may have on stood on a ridge and scanned the Bay. Impatiently, Sven encouraged him to hurry and complained that there weren't any women.

"Yackie" he called in his Swedish accent. Yackie kom igen. Nog poesi. Du sa att det fanns kvinnor här. Var?!"

"Women are in every corner Sven, but ruins like this? You may never come here again. Besides chicks dig a guy that knows a little something."

And so his friend followed Jackie's mini lecture. On the street, they bought old, souvenir post cards. Alida framed the one Jackie gave her and hung it on the wall.

It was Sunday. *Where's she getting records?* There was no Greek chorus, no messenger to answer, but he had his oracle, the sea. A few steps later, he was on Ocean Avenue. The mist permeated his being and vanquished his anguish, calmed his thinking.

It always did, and soon he felt one with it. The hundreds of sail-
ors embodied in seagulls greeted him and accompanied him on
his walk. His heart smiled when a distance down the snow-drifted
sand, he observed two boys, a scrappy red-head and chunky brunette attracting the birds by tossing scraps. Within minutes the
boys, squatting still as stones, had gained the birds' trust. The
gulls fluttered their wings and suspended themselves in the air

waves and landed tentatively nearer and nearer. Bravely, a gull
alighted on the red-head's hand. They laughed in the boisterous
cracked voices of boys high on reckless compulsion and mischief. Remembering his own care-free days, Jackie chuckled but
was interrupted by the gull's sudden, long shrill cry. The flock
circled skyward in a storm of white feathers and left the screaming bird behind. Desperately, it flapped its great wings to free
itself. The boy held tightly to its leg with one hand while guard-

ing his face with the other. His chum mocked it and howled in wicked amusement at its agitated terror. "Hey," Jackie blasted out in alarm and startled them. The chunky one dashed away, but the other paused, looked defiantly right into Jackie's face, raised the bird and then flung its face at the ground. "Don't!" he bellowed as the boy lifted the limp-gull and smashed it violently down a second time before letting its limp body drop and then ran off. Jackie raced to the gull whose soft whimpering at his feet inspired him to chase down the culprit. He caught him by his loose clothes.

"You little fucking shit!" he said and smacked both sides of his face.

"It was just a dumb bird."

"It was a seaman."

"You're crazy, old man!"

"Let me show you what it feels like to have your head slammed on the ground."

"Ow!! Let me go!!"

The boy thrashed and flailed to free himself, but Jackie had hung him upside down by one leg. He could feel his slim weight trembling in his powerful hands, and he wanted to bash his head in, but the memory of Alida admonishing him for behaving like "a barbarian," thwarted his action. Instead he sandbagged his emotions, laid him on the sand and ordered him to, "Get out of here!" Slowly the boy walked backward and a few steps away warned him, "You'll be sorry old man." He lunged forward and sent the boy sprinting away. When Jackie returned to the bird, it was obvious that it was mortally wounded. It opened one eye and squirmed in heart-wrenching agony; he stroked it. A tear ran through the lines on his wind-parched cheek. "Damn kids. Sorry my friend," he said out loud, took its slim neck in his fingers, and with a swift sharp snap mercifully ended its suffering. Though there were thousands of rocks on the beach, he took his time and selected those he thought more worthy of his twice fallen seaman's grave. The gulls danced high above the spot shrieking their lament He hurried back to the civilization side of Ocean Avenue intent on drowning the savage incident with a quick trip to the Dog, but Lowell Hunter's Mercedes roadster and the desire to hear Alida's lyrical voice drew him back to the house.

He avoided the front, slunk around the back window and peered in. Lowell and his friend Stan, in evening clothes, searched for and found glasses which they took into the living room. Jackie climbed through the window and clumped behind them startling Lowell. To Jackie, everything was wrong with the sight of him. He was holding his and Alida's volume of Aeschylus.

"What are you fops doing here?"

Lowell replied with a mocking, "Nice scarf."

"It's Alida's. Where is she?"

"Where I left her..." he paused and shot a devilish glance at Stan, "...in the bedroom."

Jackie whopped him and raised his fist again but stopped.

"Get your girly, namby-pamby asses out of here."

Lowell's choler flared, and he stood up ready to take Jackie on.

"It's not worth it," Stan told him and tugged on his jacket. Lowell checked his face for blood.

"Really Jackie, no one knows what Alida sees in you,"

"Where is she?"

"Basement... looking for a record."

"Doll?" Jackie yelled at the floor while Lowell headed out to the car.

"Titan!" she sang, "You're home early! Be right up."

The tune of her heels merrily mincing up the stairs infused him with joy and spirited him outside to meet her just as Lowell and Stan were driving off.

"Tell Mimi I'm bringing Jackie," she called after them.

While winding her grandmother's old French scarf around her, he drank in her jasmine scent and then engaged her in a long, deep, glad-to-be-back-in-your-arms kiss that would have gone on and on had they not been interrupted by the gangling young seagull murderer.

"That's him Pa!" he cried from a work truck.

He and his father, wearing a tool belt and carrying a rifle, emerged.

"You sure, Billy?"

He nodded.

Jackie's eyes bulged in disbelief and horror because he aimed the barrel at Alida.

"Leave her out of this!" he roared. "Your beef is with me!"

"What's happening, Jackie?"

"Get in the house!"

Fear had frozen her in place.

"You wanna shoot someone? Shoot me!"

Boldly, Jackie moved into the line of fire and gave her a protective, forceful nudge. Clutching the albums tightly, she bolted clumsily to a safe spot behind a column. The father approached with Billy tagging along

"Big man like you shouldn't pick on a boy?"

"Wouldn't have to if you'd taught the boy not to smash a gull to death?" Jackie moved the barrel to the side with his fingers. "You wanna fight Mac?" He held up his fists, "Come on."

"My name ain't Mac. I'm Will," he declared and gave the rifle to his son.

"Get him Pa!"

Will and Jackie circled one another in the ritualistic, ape-like moves of barroom fighters. They thrust themselves at each other simultaneously and butt heads, and then escalated into a vicious altercation. Will was a formidable match. With every landed punch, Alida winced. Billy cheered his dad on but Alida couldn't stand the violence. She left her post and clawed at Jackie to pull him off Will.

"Stop it! Stop it!"

A forgotten cigarette lighter had brought Lowell and Stan back to the house. Seeing Alida straddling Jackie, imploring the men to stop, Lowell rushed him into the living room to call the police. By the time he stepped back outside, Will was sprawled in a lifeless heap in the snow with Jackie standing over him.

"Don't worry Alida; the police are on the way."

"That was not necessary," she told Lowell and glared at him.

Jackie bent down to check on Will, but Billy read his action as a threat to his downed father. In a split second, he grit his teeth, raised the rifle, and pulled the trigger. Kaboom! Lowell jumped and scooted into the roadster. Alida shrieked over the sound of its wheels screeching off. Birds fluttered wildly. Silence fell. Finally, Will stirred.

"Pa! Pa! …. I…. I… I," Billy stammered, dropped the rifle and ran to his father.

"I'm okay," he told his son as they returned to the truck, collected the rifle and got in.

Suddenly, Jackie swooned, and Alida slipped her arm around him. He leaned on her.

"Sorry.

"Whatever for?"

"Being…you know… a barbarian."

A wave of tenderness threw her arms around him. "No, you're my hero, a real Titan. I thought he was going to shoot me."

Winded, he stumbled on the stoop and sat there with her by his side. Sirens blared on the police car up to the curb. Officer Arnie, a friend Jackie had known since grammar school, was behind the wheel. The boys at the Dog had always joked that his heft was the reason he carried out as many duties as possible without getting out of the police car. He wiggled his fingers in greeting at Alida.

"Couldn't believe it when I got a call to 361 Ocean Avenue. What's up?"

The seriousness of the situation tensed Billy and Will's faces.

"Nothing going on here Arnie."

Will exhaled a sigh of relief. Before he clunked off with Billy, he and Jackie jut their chins up at each other in acknowledgement and forgiveness.

"Figured as much. See ya down the Dog."

"You bet Arnie."

"Sit with me a minute Doll, I can't get my breath.

The lovers settled, as they often did, on the porch swing. Alida snuggled into her coat and Jackie into the comfort of her warm lap, and they stared out at the infinite sea while snowflakes tintinabulated on the ground.

"Really can't fight like I used to."

"I missed you," was all she said.

"Me too Doll," he whispered and watched as the land, the sea and the sky swirled into a phantasmagorical whirlpool, around and around it went shortening the tether that bound him to reality. A woman called "Oceanus," as a gloriously, gold and glinting wheel rolled beneath the clouds. He grounded himself by stroking Alida's arm and talking.

"Your boyfriend says nobody understands why we're together."

"Why don't you believe me? Lowell and I only went out a few times. And he doesn't understand love any more than anyone else. A few years ago no one understood Charlie Chaplin marrying that girl Oona."

"Who could? He was fifty something, and she was a little eighteen year old girl."

"And in the twenties, an American Indian man coerced a socialite into acknowledging her love for him by beating his drum every night in front of her house...every night! "

"That's a new one. And it worked?"

"It? I don't know. Love worked. Love, like the Ocean, 'reminds us humans that we are not in charge.' Love is heavenly, mysterious... star-crossed. No one understands."

Jackie squeezed her hips with his arms. Lovingly, she draped the blue scarf that across him before she read from *Prometheus.* The chariot wheels dipped back into view, and then inexplicably, he was in it as it sailed up, up, up into the troposphere. Alida's recitation paled into a faraway, lulling drone as if he were on the edge of a deep sleep, and his body became heavy on her lap; his arm flopped to the side. Folding it back across him, she saw blood on her skirt and trickling out of the corner of his mouth. Frantically, she opened his coat to find his shirt blood-drenched with a round hole in the pocket where Billy's bullet must have entered. "Jackie?" She wriggled from beneath him and darted in to call for help.

✳✳✳

The merchant ship's incessant deafening, metallic engine was roaring in his ears when he blinked his eyes open, but as soon as he saw a large-boned woman over him, he knew he was not on board.

"Who the Hell are you?" Jackie asked as her enormous hands busily bandaged his wound.

"It's me, Tethys. Fine greeting for your wife?"

"My wife? Alida is my wife."

"On earth."

"You mean…"

"Yes, brother, you were given half a century to experience mortal life and…"

"But I hadn't inhabited Jackie for fifty..."

"Jackie went and got himself killed."

Her revelation that he had left his mortal body and returned to being the God Oceanus' he was born, released tears from the corners of his eyes. Tethys placed her giant's arm on his shoulder and attempted to kiss him.

"Get away!" he cried and ordered himself to "Wake up. Wake up. Wake up! This is a hallucination. I'm Jackie, Jackie Vik! Where is Alida?"

Jackie peered over the edge of the chariot and through a hole in atmosphere. A raging blizzard was burying the ambulance into which the paramedics were sliding the stretcher on which they had placed Jackie. The mighty wind whipped off the "special

185

kinda blue" scarf. A gull snatched it from the air and he delivered it to Jackie. It was laced with Alida's scent. He buried his face in it and drank her in before he tied it securely around his neck and pleaded, "Wait!" and then cried "Alida! Alida!" So forcefull and passionate was his plea that it halted his mortal beloved in her steps by the ambulance door. She glanced around, and then raised her eyes to the grey clouds where she thought she caught a glimpse of her blue scarf.

"We gotta get going Miss," the paramedic advised her gently, and extended his hand to guide her up the step.

In the ambulance, Jackie lay unconscious, but she spoke to him anyway.

"We will be at the hospital soon."

The ambulance grumbled and sputtered and coughed for a couple of minutes before it rumbled to running and inched along Ocean Avenue, but a few feet later, it fishtailed and crashed into a snow bank with a thud. After a few minutes, Alida tapped on the window between the cab and the back.

"Can you get it started? Come on!"

Tethys gave a hearty belly laugh and pointed her finger at the scene on earth.

"What a couple of losers. Fears about losing someone or missing someone are unnecessary if you know you are immortal. Ha Ha Ha. Look at the woman. Boo Hoo."

"What do you know? You never felt anything for anyone but yourself Tethys, so. . ."

"Oceanus you are beginning to remember."

"My name is Jackie, Jackie Vik," he announced slapping his chest.

"Soon that name, that man and his experiences will only be a vague memory, and you will be glad you are not one of those weak little humans," Tethys told him with a good punch in the arm.

The ways of the gods had flooded back to Jackie, and he knew what he had to do. He collected himself, gave a hale and hearty laugh, and then he lied, "Of course, but Tethys, my dear wife and sister, I am disappointed? Tradition dictates that I transition to my former godly state in the company of my fellow Titans and gods, and my children in a great celebration. Yet here I am, alone with but selfish and negligent you. . . "

She interrupted his complaint with nervous apologies and departed to carry out her responsibilities. Jackie's thoughts drifted back to Alida now buried with the ambulance and the world around it in a massive snowstorm. To Alida's horror, the frightened, young, paramedics planned to abandon the vehicle to seek shelter in a place with an emergency generator.

Incredulous, she declared, "Leave?! You can't leave us!

"Yeah, well..."

Their minimal reply and the way they hung their heads challenged her hope that Jackie would pull through. Because the ambulance had traveled such a short distance from the house, she asked that they at least carry him there, but they deemed the task impossible for the two of them in the thigh-high snow that had accumuled. They insisted it was best for her to go and wait for them, but she was beyond convincing. She must have told them, "I will not leave Jackie," about a hundred times and assured them that she would "be all right," before they shoved their hesitancy aside and vanished behind the heavy, white winter curtain with a promise to return.

In the ambulance, Alida tended to Jackie, cooed their future plans about returning to the woods in the summer, stroked his cheek and pulled the blanket under his chin. It was then she noticed the blue scarf, her blue scarf, the one he so admired was missing. She scanned the floor and then checked for it under his shoulder.

From the chariot on high, Oceanus felt Alida's slender fingers on Jackie's face and her lips pressing against his cheek, but he was not tingling as he usually did. He knew that meant the beginning of the end of Jackie. All the bliss he had felt in being human, in loving Alida would be lost forever once his soul reintegrated with his immortal being. Though Alida had slid onto the stretcher with Jackie to warm them both in the freezing cold ambulance, he felt nothing. He watched the ghostly essence of Jackie Vik's being seep through the roof of the ambulance. He had to stop it. He wanted to stay on earth, and he had to act fast, but he was not sure what to do. Trying to solve his dilemma put so much pressure on him that he burst into a sea of tears that flooded the chariot, gushed through the atmosphere and into the clouds where he crystallized and became part of the storm. An eerie sensation pulled Alida up with a start. And she arose to fling open the ambulance. "Jackie?" she asked as a powerful flurry of damp snowflakes blew passed her face and formed a cloud over him and pressed his misty soul back into his body. Feeling foolish for allowing the cold air in, she rushed to shut the door. While she attempted to close it, he bit away his pain and struggled behind her.

"Let me help you Doll," he offered.

Alida turned to Jackie and they fell into a kiss that sent pins and needles of delight through Jackie's body and relief to Alida's heart. He leaned on her and held his bleeding gut while she helped him back to the stretcher where he collapsed and closed his eyes.

"Jackie?" she whispered with love and concern dancing in her voice.

"Right here Doll. I'm right here with you. Dry your eyes," he groaned, untied the blue scarf and handed it to her.

She laughed at herself for having allowed panic to have blinded her to it. Suddenly, the ambulance doors slammed and the engine turned over.

"Hold on back there."

"I am. Just drive," Jackie ordered and slipped his big, rough hand into Alida's.

Extracts From Adam's Diary

by
Mark Twain

From Mark Twain: "[I translated a portion of this diary some years ago, and a friend of mine printed a few copies in an incomplete form, but the public never got them. Since then I have deciphered some more of Adam's hieroglyphics, and think he has now become sufficiently important as a public character to justify this publication.]"

Extracts From Adam's Diary
by Mark Twain

MONDAY -- This new creature with the long hair is a good deal in the way. It is always hanging around and following me about. I don't like this; I am not used to company. I wish it would stay with the other animals. . . . Cloudy today, wind in the east; think we shall have rain. . . . WE? Where did I get that word-the new creature uses it.

TUESDAY -- Been examining the great waterfall. It is the finest thing on the estate, I think. The new creature calls it Niagara Falls-why, I am sure I do not know. Says it LOOKS like Niagara Falls. That is not a reason; it is mere waywardness and imbecility. I get no chance to name anything myself. The new creature names everything that comes along, before I can get in a protest. And always that same pretext is offered -- it LOOKS like the thing. There is a dodo, for instance. Says the moment one looks at it one sees at a glance that it "looks like a dodo." It will have to keep that name, no doubt. It wearies me to fret about it, and it does no good, anyway. Dodo! It looks no more like a dodo than I do.

WEDNESDAY -- Built me a shelter against the rain, but could not have it to myself in peace. The new creature intruded. When I tried to put it out it shed water out of the holes it looks with, and wiped it away with the back of its paws, and made a noise such as some of the other animals make when they are in distress. I wish it would not talk; it is always talking. That sounds like a cheap fling at the poor creature, a slur; but I do not mean it so. I have never heard the human voice before, and any new and strange sound intruding itself here upon the solemn hush of these dreaming solitudes offends my ear and seems a false note. And this new sound is so close to me; it is right at my shoulder, right at my ear, first on one side and then on the other, and I am used only to sounds that are more or less distant from me.

FRIDAY -- The naming goes recklessly on, in spite of anything I can do. I had a very good name for the estate, and it was musical and pretty -- GARDEN OF EDEN. Privately, I continue to call it that, but not any longer publicly. The new creature says it is all woods and rocks and scenery, and therefore has no resemblance to a garden. Says it LOOKS like a park, and does not look like anything BUT a park. Consequently, without consulting me, it has been new-named NIAGARA FALLS PARK. This is sufficiently high-handed, it seems to me. And already there is a sign up:

KEEP OFF THE GRASS

My life is not as happy as it was.

SATURDAY -- The new creature eats too much fruit. We are going to run short, most likely. "We" again -- that is ITS word; mine, too, now, from hearing it so much. Good deal of fog this morning. I do not go out in the fog myself. This new creature does. It goes out in all weathers, and stumps right in with its muddy feet. And talks. It used to be so pleasant and quiet here.

SUNDAY -- Pulled through. This day is getting to be more and more trying. It was selected and set apart last November as a day of rest. I had already six of them per week before. This morning found the new creature trying to clod apples out of that forbidden tree.

MONDAY -- The new creature says its name is Eve. That is all right, I have no objections. Says it is to call it by, when I want it to come. I said it was superfluous, then. The word evidently raised me in its respect; and indeed it is a large, good word and will bear repetition. It says it is not an It, it is a She. This is probably doubtful; yet it is all one to me; what she is were nothing to me if she would but go by herself and not talk.

TUESDAY -- She has littered the whole estate with execrable names and offensive signs:

THIS WAY TO THE WHIRLPOOL
THIS WAY TO GOAT ISLAND
CAVE OF THE WINDS THIS WAY

She says this park would make a tidy summer resort if there was any custom for it. Summer resort -- another invention of hers-just words, without any meaning. What is a summer resort? But it is best not to ask her, she has such a rage for explaining.

FRIDAY -- She has taken to beseeching me to stop going over the Falls. What harm does it do? Says it makes her shudder. I wonder why; I have always done it -- always liked the plunge, and coolness. I supposed it was what the Falls were for. They have no other use that I can see, and they must have been made for something. She says they were only made for scenery -- like the rhinoceros and the mastodon.

I went over the Falls in a barrel -- not satisfactory to her. Went over in a tub -- still not satisfactory. Swam the Whirlpool and the Rapids in a fig-leaf suit. It got much damaged. Hence, tedious complaints about my extravagance. I am too much hampered here. What I need is a change of scene.

SATURDAY -- I escaped last Tuesday night, and traveled two days, and built me another shelter in a secluded place, and obliterated my tracks as well as I could, but she hunted me out by means of a beast which she has tamed and calls a wolf, and came making that pitiful noise again, and shedding that water out of the places she looks with. I was obliged to return with her, but will presently emigrate again when occasion offers. She engages herself in many foolish things; among others; to study out why the animals called lions and tigers live on grass and flowers, when, as she says, the sort of teeth they wear would indicate that they were intended to eat each other. This is foolish, because to do that would be to kill each other, and that would introduce what, as I understand, is called "death"; and death, as I have been told, has not yet entered the Park. Which is a pity, on some accounts.

SUNDAY -- Pulled through.

MONDAY -- I believe I see what the week is for: it is to give time to rest up from the weariness of Sunday. It seems a good idea. . . . She has been climbing that tree again. Clodded her out of it. She said nobody was looking. Seems to consider that a sufficient justification for chancing any dangerous thing. Told her that. The word justification moved her admiration -- and envy, too, I thought. It is a good word.

TUESDAY -- She told me she was made out of a rib taken from my body. This is at least doubtful, if not more than that. I have not missed any rib. . . . She is in much trouble about the buzzard; says grass does not agree with it; is afraid she can't raise it; thinks it was intended to live on decayed flesh. The buzzard must get along the best it can with what is provided. We cannot overturn the whole scheme to accommodate the buzzard.

SATURDAY -- She fell in the pond yesterday when she was looking at herself in it, which she is always doing. She nearly strangled, and said it was most uncomfortable. This made her sorry for the creatures which live in there, which she calls fish, for she continues to fasten names on to things that don't need them and don't come when they are called by them, which is a matter of no consequence to her, she is such a numbskull, anyway; so she got a lot of them out and brought them in last night and put them in my bed to keep warm, but I have noticed them now and then all day and I don't see that they are any happier there then they were before, only quieter. When night comes I shall throw them outdoors. I will not sleep with them again, for I find them clammy and unpleasant to lie among when a person hasn't anything on.

SUNDAY -- Pulled through.

TUESDAY -- She has taken up with a snake now. The other animals are glad, for she was always experimenting with them and bothering them; and I am glad because the snake talks, and this enables me to get a rest.

FRIDAY -- She says the snake advises her to try the fruit of the tree, and says the result will be a great and fine and noble education. I told her there would be another result, too -- it would introduce death into the world. That was a mistake -- it had been better to keep the remark to myself; it only gave her an idea -- she could save the sick buzzard, and furnish fresh meat to the despondent lions and tigers. I advised her to keep away from the tree. She said she wouldn't. I foresee trouble. Will emigrate.

WEDNESDAY -- I have had a variegated time. I escaped last night, and rode a horse all night as fast as he could go, hoping to get clear of the Park and hide in some other country before the trouble should begin; but it was not to be. About an hour after sun-up, as I was riding through a flowery plain where thousands of animals were grazing, slumbering, or playing with each other, according to their wont, all of a sudden they broke into a tempest of frightful noises, and in one moment the plain was a frantic commotion and every beast was destroying its neighbor. I knew what it meant-Eve had eaten that fruit, and death was come into the world. . . . The tigers ate my house, paying no attention when I ordered them to desist, and they would have eaten me if I had stayed-which I didn't, but went away in much haste. . . . I found this place, outside the Park, and was fairly comfortable for a few days, but she has found me out. Found me out, and has named the place Tonawanda-says it LOOKS like that. In fact I was not sorry she came, for there are but meager pickings here, and she brought some of those apples. I was obliged to eat them, I was so hungry. It was against my principles, but I find that principles have no real force except when one is well fed. . . . She came curtained in boughs and bunches of leaves, and when I asked her what she meant by such nonsense, and snatched them away and threw them down, she tittered and blushed. I had never seen a person titter and blush before, and to me it seemed unbecoming and idiotic. She said I would soon know how it was myself. This was correct. Hungry as I was, I laid down the apple half-eaten -- certainly the best one I ever saw, considering the lateness of the season-and arrayed myself in the discarded boughs and branches, and then spoke to her with some severity and ordered her to go and get some more and not make a spectacle or herself. She did it, and after this we crept down to where the wild-beast battle had been, and collected some skins, and I made her patch together a couple of suits proper for public occasions. They are uncomfortable, it is true, but stylish, and that is the main point about clothes. . . . I find she is a good deal of a companion. I see I should be lonesome and depressed without her, now that I have lost my property. Another thing, she says it is ordered that we work for our living hereafter. She will be useful. I will superintend.

TEN DAYS LATER -- She accuses ME of being the cause of our disaster! She says, with apparent sincerity and truth, that the Serpent assured her that the forbidden fruit was not apples, it was chestnuts. I said I was innocent, then, for I had not eaten any chestnuts. She said the Serpent informed her that "chestnut" was a figurative term meaning an aged and moldy joke. I turned pale at that, for I have made many jokes to pass the weary time, and some of them could have been of that sort, though I had honestly supposed that they were new when I made them. She asked me if I had made one just at the time of the catastrophe. I was obliged to admit that I had made one to myself, though not aloud. It was this. I was thinking about the Falls, and I said to myself, "How wonderful it is to see that vast body of water tumble down there!" Then in an instant a bright thought flashed into my head, and I let it fly, saying, "It would be a deal more wonderful to see it tumble UP there!" -- and I was just about to kill myself with laughing at it when all nature broke loose in war and death and I had to flee for my life. "There," she said, with triumph, "that is just it; the Serpent mentioned that very jest, and called it the First Chestnut, and said it was coeval with the creation." Alas, I am indeed to blame. Would that I were not witty; oh, that I had never had that radiant thought!

NEXT YEAR -- We have named it Cain. She caught it while I was up country trapping on the North Shore of the Erie; caught it in the timber a couple of miles from our dug-out -- or it might have been four, she isn't certain which. It resembles us in some ways, and may be a relation. That is what she thinks, but this is an error, in my judgment. The difference in size warrants the conclusion that it is a different and new kind of animal -- a fish, perhaps, though when I put it in the water to see, it sank, and she plunged in and snatched it out before there was opportunity for the experiment to determine the matter. I still think it is a fish, but she is indifferent about what it is, and will not let me have it to try. I do not understand this. The coming of the creature seems to have changed her whole nature and made her unreasonable about experiments. She thinks more of it than she does of any of the other animals, but is not able to explain why. Her mind is disordered -- everything shows it. Sometimes she carries the fish in her arms half the night when it complains and wants to get to the water. At such times the water comes out of the places in her face that she looks out of, and she pats the fish on the back and makes soft sounds with her mouth to soothe it, and betrays sorrow and solicitude in a hundred ways. I have never seen her do like this with any other fish, and it troubles me greatly. She used to carry the young tigers around so, and play with them, before we lost our property, but it was only play; she never took on about them like this when their dinner disagreed with them.

SUNDAY -- She doesn't work, Sundays, but lies around all tired out, and likes to have the fish wallow over her; and she makes fool noises to amuse it, and pretends to chew its paws, and that makes it laugh. I have not seen a fish before that could laugh. This makes me doubt. . . . I have come to like Sunday myself. Superintending all the week tires a body so. There ought to be more Sundays. In the old days they were tough, but now they come handy.

WEDNESDAY -- It isn't a fish. I cannot quite make out what it is. It makes curious devilish noises when not satisfied, and says "goo-goo" when it is. It is not one of us, for it doesn't walk; it is not a bird, for it doesn't fly; it is not a frog, for it doesn't hop; it is not a snake, for it doesn't crawl; I feel sure it is not a fish, though I cannot get a chance to find out whether it can swim or not. It merely lies around, and mostly on its back, with its feet up. I have not seen any other animal do that before. I said I believed it was an enigma; but she only admired the word without understanding it. In my judgment it is either an enigma or some king of a bug. If it dies, I will take it apart and see what its arrangements are. I never had a thing perplex me so.

THREE MONTHS LATER -- The perplexity augments instead of diminishing. I sleep but little. It has ceased from lying around, and goes about on its four legs now. Yet it differs from the other four legged animals, in that its front legs are unusually short, consequently this causes the main part of its person to stick up uncomfortably high in the air, and this is not attractive. It is built much as we are, but its method of traveling shows that it is not of our breed. The short front legs and long hind ones indicate that it is of the kangaroo family, but it is a marked variation of that species, since the true kangaroo hops, whereas this one never does. Still it is a curious and interesting variety, and has not been catalogued before. As I discovered it, I have felt justified in securing the credit of the discovery by attaching my name to it, and hence have called it KANGAROORUM ADAMIENSIS.... It must have been a young one when it came, for it has grown exceedingly since. It must be five times as big, now, as it was then, and when discontented it is able to make from twenty-two to thirty-eight times the noise it made at first. Coercion does not modify this, but has the contrary effect. For this reason I discontinued the system. She reconciles it by persuasion, and by giving it things which she had previously told me she wouldn't give it. As already observed, I was not at home when it first came, and she told me she found it in the woods. It seems odd that it should be the only one, yet it must be so, for I have worn myself out these many weeks trying to find another one to add to my collection, and for this to play with; for surely then it would be quieter and we could tame it more easily. But I find none, nor any vestige of any; and strangest of all, no tracks. It has to live on the ground, it cannot help itself; therefore, how does it get about without leaving a track? I have set a dozen traps, but they do no good. I catch all small animals except that one; animals that merely go into the trap out of curiosity, I think, to see what the milk is there for. They never drink it.

THREE MONTHS LATER -- The Kangaroo still continues to grow, which is very strange and perplexing. I never knew one to be so long getting its growth. It has fur on its head now; not like kangaroo fur, but exactly like our hair except that it is much finer and softer, and instead of being black is red. I am like to lose my mind over the capricious and harassing developments of this unclassifiable zoological freak. If I could catch another one -- but that is hopeless; it is a new variety, and the only sample; this is plain. But I caught a true kangaroo and brought it in, thinking that this one, being lonesome, would rather have that for company than have no kin at all, or any animal it could feel a nearness to or get sympathy from in its forlorn condition here among strangers who do not know its ways or habits, or what to

do to make it feel that it is among friends; but it was a mistake --
it went into such fits at the sight of the kangaroo that I was convinced it had never seen one before. I pity the poor noisy little
animal, but there is nothing I can do to make it happy. If I could
tame it -- but that is out of the question; the more I try the worse
I seem to make it. It grieves me to the heart to see it in its little
storms of sorrow and passion. I wanted to let it go, but she
wouldn't hear of it. That seemed cruel and not like her; and yet
she may be right. It might be lonelier than ever; for since I cannot find another one, how could IT?

FIVE MONTHS LATER -- It is not a kangaroo. No, for it sup-
ports itself by holding to her finger, and thus goes a few steps on
its hind legs, and then falls down. It is probably some kind of a
bear; and yet it has no tail -- as yet -- and no fur, except upon its
head. It still keeps on growing -- that is a curious circumstance,
for bears get their growth earlier than this. Bears are dangerous-
since our catastrophe -- and I shall not be satisfied to have this
one prowling about the place much longer without a muzzle on.
I have offered to get her a kangaroo if she would let this one go,
but it did no good -- she is determined to run us into all sorts of
foolish risks, I think. She was not like this before she lost her
mind.

A FORTNIGHT LATER -- I examined its mouth. There is no
danger yet: it has only one tooth. It has no tail yet. It makes more
noise now than it ever did before -- and mainly at night. I have
moved out. But I shall go over, mornings, to breakfast, and see if
it has more teeth. If it gets a mouthful of teeth it will be time for
it to go, tail or no tail, for a bear does not need a tail in order to
be dangerous.

FOUR MONTHS LATER -- I have been off hunting and fishing a month, up in the region that she calls Buffalo; I don't know
why, unless it is because there are not any buffaloes there. Meantime the bear has learned to paddle around all by itself on its
hind legs, and says "poppa" and "momma." It is certainly a new
species. This resemblance to words may be purely accidental, of

course, and may have no purpose or meaning; but even in that case it is still extraordinary, and is a thing which no other bear can do. This imitation of speech, taken together with general absence of fur and entire absence of tail, sufficiently indicates that this is a new kind of bear. The further study of it will be exceedingly interesting. Meantime I will go off on a far expedition among the forests of the north and make an exhaustive search. There must certainly be another one somewhere, and this one will be less dangerous when it has company of its own species. I will go straightway; but I will muzzle this one first.

THREE MONTHS LATER -- It has been a weary, weary hunt, yet I have had no success. In the mean time, without stirring from the home estate, she has caught another one! I never saw such luck. I might have hunted these woods a hundred years, I never would have run across that thing.

NEXT DAY -- I have been comparing the new one with the old one, and it is perfectly plain that they are of the same breed. I was going to stuff one of them for my collection, but she is prejudiced against it for some reason or other; so I have relinquished the idea, though I think it is a mistake. It would be an irreparable loss to science if they should get away. The old one is tamer than it was and can laugh and talk like a parrot, having learned this, no doubt, from being with the parrot so much, and having the imitative faculty in a high developed degree. I shall be astonished if it turns out to be a new kind of parrot; and yet I ought not to be astonished, for it has already been everything else it could think of since those first days when it was a fish. The new one is as ugly as the old one was at first; has the same sulphur-and-raw-meat complexion and the same singular head without any fur on it. She calls it Abel.

TEN YEARS LATER –

They are BOYS; we found it out long ago. It was their coming in that small immature shape that puzzled us; we were not used to it. There are some girls now. Abel is a good boy, but if Cain had stayed a bear it would have improved him. After all these years, I see that I was mistaken about Eve in the beginning; it is better to live outside the Garden with her than inside it without her. At first I thought she talked too much; but now I should be sorry to have that voice fall silent and pass out of my life. Blessed be the chestnut that brought us near together and taught me to know the goodness of her heart and the sweetness of her spirit!

FORTY YEARS LATER

It is my prayer, it is my longing, that we may pass from this life together—a longing which shall never perish from the earth, but shall have place in the heart of every wife that loves, until the end of time; and it shall be called by my name.

***

At Eve's Grave
ADAM: Wheresoever she was, THERE was Eden.

Poems

List of Poems

Something to Nothing
Girl
Déjà Vu I know you
Wedding Ring Slipped off my Finger
Tuesday's Destiny
My Darling's Darling I'm not
Mr. Know it All
Signs
Ode to flirtin'
Green girls blue are golden
Sinner Sinner
Mis-Matched Matches
Ride to the Picnic
The Couple
Box of Stars, Box of Moonlight
Dictator
Reborn
Tall, Blonde, Chinese
Odd Condoms by the River
Frustration
Fish Fillay [sic]
Between the Ring Dings & the Ding Dongs
Tick Tock O'clock

Something to Nothing

How strange.
How wonderful.
There is something
to this nothingness between us.
Let's promise never to find it,
so we won't be able to lose it.
It doesn't weigh like led.
It doesn't' weigh like tissue.
It is a small bird in the palm of a hand.
It has a pulse.
It can fly away.

How strange.
How wonderful.
How incredible
the vast sophistication
the utterly fantastic
complicated simplicity
of something that is nothing
between us.

Girl

Slim, pretty coquette
winsome, mirthful girl
radiating youth from
the toes of wobbly new stilettos
to everywhere glancing heads
cascading a frame around your face,
chestnut hair, flipped over your shoulder
with inexperienced fingers dipped in red
they slide down your ribs to your waist
and rest on your inchoate hips turning
and swiveling you hypnotic by me.

The room is intoxicated with
the dew of your exuberant elixir
cast subconsciously in naked coyness.
Your playful available flirt's nervous,
too loudly delivered, at once forgiven
by the grace of your elegant arms
and charmingly, goofy guffaw
as you stumble and try to look cool.
Linger near, linger here,
let me undress you with my eyes
and run my fingers over the contour
of your tantalizing naïveté
and supple silhouette responding
in the obscene raunch of my mind.
Please don't unbutton your coat
with the dark lining or empty its
pockets of their complications.
inflate me
with your flashing eyes

and attentive airs
lead me on with your hand pressed on my chest
over my racing heart.
Violate my space with your breath
speak softly so close to my face
that your eyelashes whisper on my cheek;
then offer up some vigorous "Hey"
to some someone over there from your life
and saunter freshly away.

Déjà Vu

At the crossroads of rain and nowhere
in the vacated post-lunch hush,
above the beer weathered wood
a cheeseburger and consommé
for two strangers dressed in
loneliness and damp corduroy
sitting and waiting out the rain
were filled with that eerie
feeling, déjà vu, I know you
as soon as their eyes met
they scanned each others faces
and exchanged a smile
while he smoothed his hair
she toyed with her glass
and they began that game
discovering where they
must have met before
foregoing the prelude
of intros and small talk
impulsively blurting
friends' names and universities
concerts and New Years parties
a rush of conceivable possibilities
entertainingly exhausted
left them grinning achingly
with his hand or her forearm
by the soup never tasted
and a quixotic conclusion
to feeling déjà vu, I know you
and the enchanting magnetic attraction
was in a remnant, a unit of heredity
carried forward for years, maybe centuries.

in the vacated post-lunch hush
nascent tree buds thirsty quaffed
spring's cool polyphonic raindrops
pattering sonorously on doves' eves
sparking brightly off umbrellas' canopies
whose owners pause for the fragrance
of dewy Heaven Scent Magnolia trees
while the long-ago lovers playfully
pondered the possible mystery
miming who they might have been
wearing a golden pocket watch
silently telling time in a brocade vest
or a corseted waist narrowed below
a décolleté neckline plunging a full hand
she allowed his measuring with his palm
flattened warmly on her rising chest
their inner visions in synch and in tune
their inner thighs in furtive contact
strangers steamy stirring intimately
Ulysses once more with Penelope
Cleopatra with her Mark Anthony
Emperor Napoleon and his Countess Marie
reincarnated, souls remembering
rekindling imprinted passion
or merely two strangers dressed in
loneliness and damp corduroy
sitting and waiting out the rain
at a confluence of past present and future

Wedding Ring Slipped off My Finger

Wedding ring slipped off my finger
wrapped around my throat
tethering me to an unmagic place
where duets not yet written
waited to be sung
where words not yet phrased
waited to be spoken
in a home, not a house,
where we feathered roosted
and love could have grown
had the windows been opened
for each of us to soar away
explore our boundaries
not to escape but to yearn
for the intimate familiarity of we,

a pair perched amorous sublime
sharing uncommon experiences
as lovebirds do.
Had the windows been opened
our harmonious descant
would zephyr along
the energy of everyone,
from everywhere we knew
and places we didn't
not caged in a house, not a home,
muffled in heavy curtains
tense with drama and tears
with limits and fears
tightening the golden tether
around my throat
prohibiting my view

inhibiting my breathing,
oxygen to my brain,
sustenance to
my soul
should have been waxing
with yours,
not shackled.
Things to do dis-incarcerate me
for brief, long hours of time
to turn and twist and tug at
this wedding ring
slipped off my finger.

Tuesday's Destiny

far away as the snow from June
far away as a hawk from the moon
time unraveled your Thursday's destiny
a dim distance some many miles from
me dwelling, left here -- dwelling right there,
close in your square rumpled cotton pocket
barely visible in sheets modestly spread
loose loving limbs only sensual shapes
flash a luscious-lipped split second smile
folded now perspiration damp Kodak paper
disposable indispensable image
habitually checked on by your fingertips
meaningless without your mind,
without your eyes' returning gaze at me
from your head; lazy sleepy morning air
redolent with those forget-me-not roses
red wine in long-stemmed goblets half drunk
you flashed a manly-uninhibited nude
goodbye pose on softened linens unslept in

already missing your restless weight
your scent lingering on every thread
right there with you that is left here with me
on the firm pillows downy with our dreams
crinkled now perspiration damp Kodak paper
disposable indispensable image
habitually smoothed by my fingertips
meaningless without my mind
rendering tangible your firm sinewy contour
nestled as near as the sun to noon
as near as lyrics to a tune

running breathlessly round and round
during hours and hours of
cleaning, working, talking,
sauntering slowly shopping reluctant by 'till
time unravels your next Tuesday's destiny
up the stairs, through the door and back to us
back to we, back to Tuesday's destiny.

My Darling's Darling I'm not

My darling's darling I am not
for his love is all women
all women who are dreamers
because he is unwittingly a dream.

His size announces his strength
as he slowly parades toward them
offering their hoped for
"Where have you been all my life?"
or some other cliché
his soft voice shouts
his gentleness in their ears
before casually placing a firm hand
bragging of experience
not only on a thigh
but beneath their skirts not held in place.

Unappreciated or even noticed
as a woman for so long
the female dreamer
goes on dreaming that
he will take her face in
his hands and kiss her.
 This the dream does.
 Then stops.
Her lips are resistant
with her sudden morals
he kisses away
her coquettish objections
follows his instincts

and my darling
carries her off into her sunset
at least in her mind.

My darling's darling I am not
for his love is all women,
all women who are dreamers
because my darling is unwittingly
a dream.

Mr. Know it All
(For Bob)

Never Guessing
Mr. Know it All
didn't know it all.
He was worshipped
because he knew everything.
But he didn't know
the one last thing
he needed to know to be
"all knowing," and
he didn't want to know it
because he knew he would
go insane
knowing it all.

so he ran away from his inner self
by skulking his outer self
in designer label men's wear
and striking **GQ** poses
in intercontinental hotels
where each week they changed the
menu's international dish and
the costume of the
garcon-ober-waitress
transporting him
1000 leagues around the world
from a blasé café chair
no seatbelt, no film, no destination
but "fat city"
for the already vacationing owner
who raised the minimum to $5.00
which all who were "in the know,"

agreed was fare to sit there.

And sitting there
in a cache of smoke
in the interlude between
Hungarian goulash and French Pastry
the final mortal blow of knowledge
simply crossed his mind
transforming him into
an enlightened maniac
who took the check and gave the waitress this tip,
"Do yourself a favor. Stay stupid beautiful."

Signs

(For John: April 25, 2005 3:00)

What'll I do about you
who knocks at my door
with gentle hands & voice
summoning amity and play
sitting near, breath to breath, so close
you're blind to my posted signs:
SOLICITORS UNWELCOME
NO LOITERING - GONE FISHING
you persist, unwittingly insist
my persona respond, not resist by
unearthing my mind, mining my smile.
I blush and find a jacket useless
The rainy April day
suddenly no colder than a
moonless June at noon on the beach.
Though my psyche is in pieces
the ache is soothed by the titillating stream
of kindness. thoughtful intelligence
and flattering trifles your lips
spout and honey over me.
Tempted, I see myself clearly in
the glass café door
reflecting foolish, girlish, coquettish
my signs clearly posted:
SOLICITORS UNWELCOME
NO LOITERING - GONE FISHING
reflecting delible, melting and lopsided.
What'll I do about you?

Ode to flirtin'

Fancifree flirtin'
a thing to do.
And if I had my druthers
we'd never get to know one another
me and you.
We'd forever just meet in bars
along the Avenue
Not have to
Not must to
Just happen to
whenever we have the time.

For fancifree flirtin's
a thing to do.
No porcelain passions
for me and you.
No broken promises.
No tears to dry only you and I
perfunctorily, painlessly playfully
doing nothing muching
about getting closer together.
Just fancifree flirtin' a thing to do.

And if I had my druthers,
and I think I do,
we'd never get to know one another
me and you.
And we'll have a perfect relationship
never ending,
never having begun.
Fancifree flirtin's
harmless grown-up fun.

Green girls blue are golden

Nursing drinks
riding barstools
the way they used to Daddy's shoulders
green girls are playing games
unchaperoned
watched by
their mothers' warnings
they mind
their manners
are in the way
at the game of chance
in the recreation room
of the night school of experience
answering "yes," mischievously
short-sheeting their own beds
by doing the boy's next door
for a laugh
crying when the fable's end
is sad
not happy
as it was when Gramma read it
for the last of countless times
7300 evenings ago
when life first began
imitating art
now found untrue
from a philosophical point of view
discovered at the bottom of drinks
bought by possible next men
last seen on the last page
somewhere near "...happily ever after."

Green girls blue are golden
drowning mothers' voices
the barstool wanders off the path
and the fable forgotten
ENDS

Sinner Sinner

sinner sinner-
sinner on a
bed of flames
licking at my flesh
burning with desire
temptation and urges
form a pyre to destroy resistance

didn't know what fire
our touching would ignite
didn't know we would
burn so bright as to
invite the devil to cast us
in a blaze
of lust's delight

white hot heavenly bodies
shapely naked in the night
are also enormous shadows
on the walls
in the dark
flashing, sparking, touchwood
lapping our writhing being
with luminous tongues
panting, stroking
along our torsos gloriously
from limb to limb to limb
sinner sinner-
sinner on a
bed of flames
going insane
kindling the devil again and again

willingly remaining in the flames
on a pool of smoking sheets
incinerating decency
degrading us to ashes
there's no way out but up
in the smoke
like an ancient phoenix
didn't know the fire
we would light

Mis-matched Matches

Mis matched matches
don't ignite
in pretension fogged restaurants.
Sparks die
as the sulfite laced
wine fades,
but the mis-matched
insist on trying to
strike up conversation
... again,
this time on their books,
his from the "B" girl joint
hers from the French library.
they bend and strike and
bend and strike
and bend
and strike
out
AGAIN,
nearly breaking off their
silly mis-minded heads
scratching and having
bent beneath pretension.
By admitting their differences
their hands
hang closer together
and touch
involuntarily struck -
they light up.

Ride to the Picnic

Worn black leather straddled
The seat
riding her to the picnic.
She held on
For balance
as they bounced
over the curb,
her laughter in the wind blowing
with his unmuffled ego thundering
in counterpoint
and they appeared but in sound
to those asleep under feather downs
behind rattling windows.
Searching for
her smile of ready
in his rear view mirror
he adored her kid skin cheek.

Silently with a twisting
detonation
they syncopated distance
thrusting themselves
into the wind leaving
it ripped and tattered behind
all the way to the vanishing point
of a curious neighbor's perspective
before eaning left
into the sunrise
in love in perfect
picnic symmetry.

The Couple

Each went to the party
for the sake of going somewhere,
anywhere to ward off loneliness,
chance newfound companionship.
They were the only ones without dates.
He wore glasses and
she wore her heart on the sleeve
of her daringly backless copied original
shimmering in the effervescent
mood-light that softened its creases
and a thread on his jacket
as well as their anxieties and insecurities,
but it
illuminated innuendoes
flirtatious raised eyebrows
and stolen mutual glances of attraction.
One long gaze brought
midnight's possibility into view:
when at last they were introduced
"How do you do?"
Precede, "Where are you from?"
And of course, "What do you do?"
And banter about how
much each likes the
other's eyes or shoes.

72 1/2 kisses, 301 thrusts,
and at least one gratifying
roar of ecstasy
before dawn unveils the sunrise
glowing in the window near
his bed, or will it be hers,

never truly slept in?

And then what?
Wait for the next party
for the sake of going somewhere,
anywhere to ward off loneliness?

right in the middle of one last dance
the only ones without dates
decided it is not,
recited about the 119th line
of the night,
begged off with respective responsibilities
exchange kisses on the cheek
and disappeared.

Box of Stars, Box of Moonlight

They're gazing at you; they're wishing on me.
Night's nothing but flat black without us
So I'm waiting in a doorway slowly fading of sun
Waiting softly for you to come
Cuz you've got a box of moonlight
And I've got a box of stars
for the sky approaching indigo
Indigo
Indigo
Indigo
Indigone

We are the lights
We'll make it bright
Make the nights are our days!
We're stealing; we're streaming
we're shooting right into the dark
breaking through window panes
in blades, in shafts, in rays.
I'll dance on steel guitar strings
You'll dance naked on salty shoulders
Mingle with me sweetly on the bar
I'll burst white in the mirror

I feel you coming
I know you're coming, coming soon.
Night's nothing but flat black without us
So I'm waiting in a doorway slowly fading of sun
Waiting for you to come
Cuz you've got a box of moonlight

And I've got a box of stars
Yes, you've got a box of moonlight
And I've got a box of stars
a box of stars
a box of stars
a box of stars

The Dictator

I wanted to look away.
I wanted to be stronger
I wanted to run!
I had heard
He was a Dictator
In an army of one
in the undeclared
sexual revolution
uniformed in an old black sweater
and tight leather pants
slid as tightly as his own skin
over his sinewy legs that
ran straight and strong right up to
his powerful narrow hips
and broad shoulders
where a girl would rest her feet
and enjoy his face
angular and experienced.

Already a platoon of
female recruits knew
that a golden peace sign…
cool to the touch
slid back and forth across
his chest
and the words "free" and "love"
were tattooed in blue but
often lipsticked in red
on his upper thigh.
Though acting alone he had
powerful support for
he had been deployed by

234

Himeros, the Greek God of desire,
to carry out his orders
to awaken the world's senses
to liberate it from
lackluster carnality and
blasé missionary intimacy.

His confident gait was
a moving violation
with which he commanded
attention along with
his steely, smug gaze
seductive enough to
render his prey volunteers
to be captured
taken to close closed quarters
subjected to his lusty wiles
and imprisoned by his arms.
I wanted to look away.
I wanted to be stronger
I wanted to run.

Reborn

(For Kémeu)

I was dying while living
almost unconscious
until the music
of your black cowboy boots
and your big brains
oozed down on me
and woke me up
with some song
philosophy you spoke
some sweet lyrics you wrote
and sang melodies softly to me
while I was reading books
you placed in my hands
referring me to Alan Watts
and Jim Morrison of years ago
denying Christ, embracing sexuality.
I came to realize
I am living while dying
for more music to pour
down on me and
arouse me ethereally
from this drowsy winter still life
to abet an orgasm of Spring
slip me off my seat to
run my hands through
the ragged black poetry of your hair
and rise me up on tippy toe for
your mouth mine to melt
into the universe
your body mine to thrill with an

infusion of fluid stars,
I am fully conscious, alert now
helplessly nestling you
comfortably unfamiliar delectable
and doing a new our bodies harmonize.

Please! Don't! Stop!
Please don't stop.
drench me, soak me, drown me
in your milky way.
Slaked, satisfied, finished.
Dust to dust
thoughts of dying
vanquished by lust
and the music of black cowboy boots,
I am hanging crazy from your shadow
I am not dying; I am not living;
I am reborn.

Tall, Blonde, Chinese

I am who I am
I never was good at
pretending anybody else.
I know
I've tried.
It was for love.
Be taller asked one first.
So I put on heels.
He ran away
with someone barely 5' tall.
Be blonde said one next,
and I will never let you go.
So I tinted my hair.
He flirted with brunettes thereafter.
Be Chinese demanded one last,
not even death will part us.
So I carefully painted my eyes.
He fell deeply in love
with someone else
pretending to be me.

Odd Condoms by the River

Odd condoms by the river
spilling seeds not disseminated
gooey, warm and pathetic
in the coming sun
seeds unable to reach fertile ground
lying on the pollinated earth
beneath a willow and a blooming tree
There are better place they could be
cozy in a bed
slippery in an esophagus
an accidental late night snack
flirting with mischievous eggs
in a soft, warm womb.

Odd condoms
discarded by the river
their love-glove luster drying
their powerfully virile contents dying
are little reminders
of the necessity of precaution
stifled impulsiveness
furtive, licentious night life
naughty, but safe meaningless sex.
Or was it true love
that filled the receptacle tip
with an unknown president who
won't lead us to war
an artist who won't suffer
or a lover who won't come
won't toss condoms by the river?

Frustration

His heart beats in his pants
so he beats his
pounding head on the wall
trying to get any
from anyone
trying to get some
from the blonde down the hall
whose good looks beat all
when she walks in the streets
he beats the table at night
with his drumstick
looking for somewhere to
muffle his pounding heart
giving him away on Mondays
when young secretaries come in
beat from sexy Saturday nights
and all they want to do is
talk about it.
A siren screams in the street below.
"Gimmie a little peace," he hollers
tossing her a glance which she
unexpectedly returns
slicing the frosty night air
his heart jumps in his throat.
He grabs his head
and beats it with his hand

Fish Fillay [sic]

He loved shopping at her fish market
spending thousands of seconds looking
spending himself dry, again and again
until she was happily exhausted
until rapture for the final sale
brought her chestnut awning
cascading down in front of her eyes.

She loved to watch him shopping
losing his mind over fish slowly
admiring and contemplating
sniffing,
taking his time,
fondling this,
feeling that
sampling without asking
glistening dark pink, flesh
and though cloyed, he would
always succumb to her charms once more
finally giving her all her had
for one last piece of fresh raw fillay.

Between the Ring Dings & Ding Dongs

They stood near the curb
in the sun
buttoning their coats
adjusting their packages
in their arms
They didn't know it
but their affair had already begun
in the store,
between the Ring Dings and the Ding Dongs
where a loaf of bread had tumbled,
and they both reached out to catch it
and their fingers touched
and their eyes met
and they chuckled nervously
and couldn't look away.
For a split second
they searched one another's faces
for familiarity and momentarily
the dull drone of the cash register stopped.
Someone pushing by, broke the spell
and she nested the bread on the shelf
before leaving
glancing over her shoulder at him
intently studying a bag of chips.
Just as she looked away,
he looked up
and saw her departing.

She rushed for the light...missed it.
Rushed for the tram...missed it.

242

Rushed for the bus…missed it.
Decided to walk
and stepped back on the curb
with the crowd waiting to cross
the street.
Sighing a frustrated sigh
a chip crunched and crumbled
onto her hair and shoulder.
Annoyed she turned
to see him, the one from
between the Ring Dings and the Ding Dongs
where a loaf of bread had tumbled,
and they smiled.

Tick Tock

Tick-tock.
The time is seven…ho hum, ho hum, and
I will color you this hour.
I will color you grey this hour;
sadly grey, languidly grey, grey-suited
for that is the color of the early mornings
of little boys who must be men
by break of day…ho hum, ho hum Tick-tock

Tick-tock.
The time is noon….Chomp-chomp sip; chomp-chomp sip.
I will color you this hour.
I will color you lavender this hour
hurriedly lavender, rushingly lavender, lavender-eyed
for that is the color
of the whites of blue-eyed big city debauchers
dashingly dapper dining who must get back soon.
Chomp-chomp sip. Chomp-chomp, sip. Tick-tock

Tick-tock
The time is six hot licks, hot licks and
I will color you this hour.
I will color you turquoise
rudely turquoise, lewdly turquoise, turquoise nude
for that is the color
of boys in men's bodies
ferreting females, fondling fancies
who must be loved to live.
hot licks, hot licks
Tick-tock.

End

Tabatne Keihtánit

MORE ABOUT AUTHOR WINCHINCHALA

https://www.facebook.com/peoplwithwings [sic]

http://www.barnesandnoble.com/s/WINCHINCHALA

http://www.peoplewithwingspublishing.blogspot.com

If you purchased a misreleased proof of any book, contact People With Wings

peoplewithwings@gmail.com

Write "Exchange" in the subject line. Details will be sent on how to return it for the new second edition.

www.ingramcontent.com/pod-product-compliance
Lightning Source LLC
LaVergne TN
LVHW011345080426
835511LV00005B/130